COLORING BOOK
FOR ADULTS

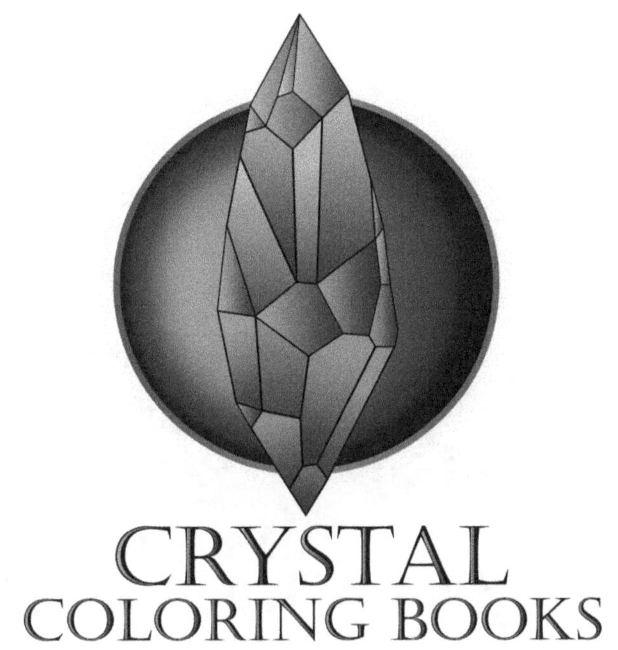

CRYSTAL
COLORING BOOKS

ISBN: 9781724103550

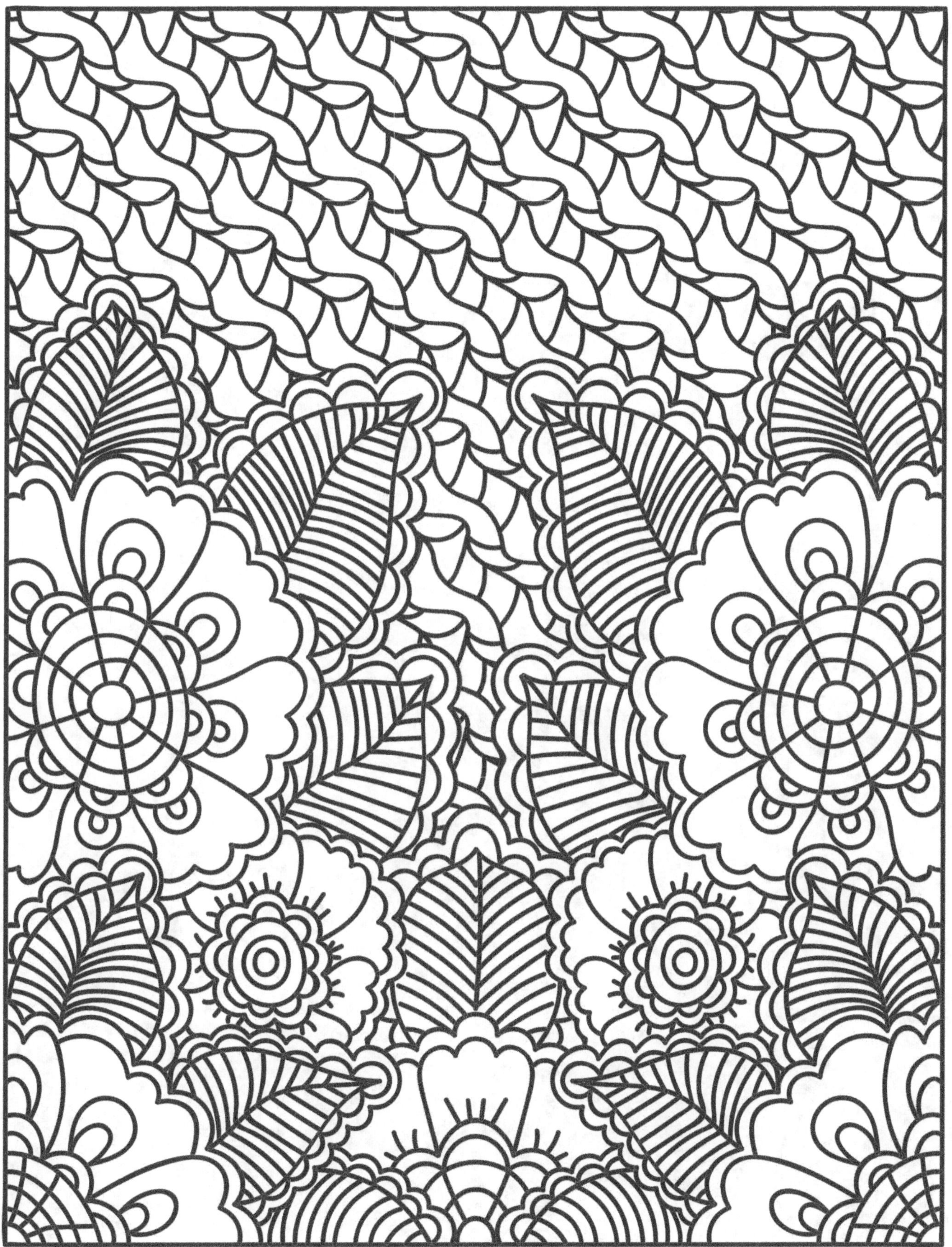

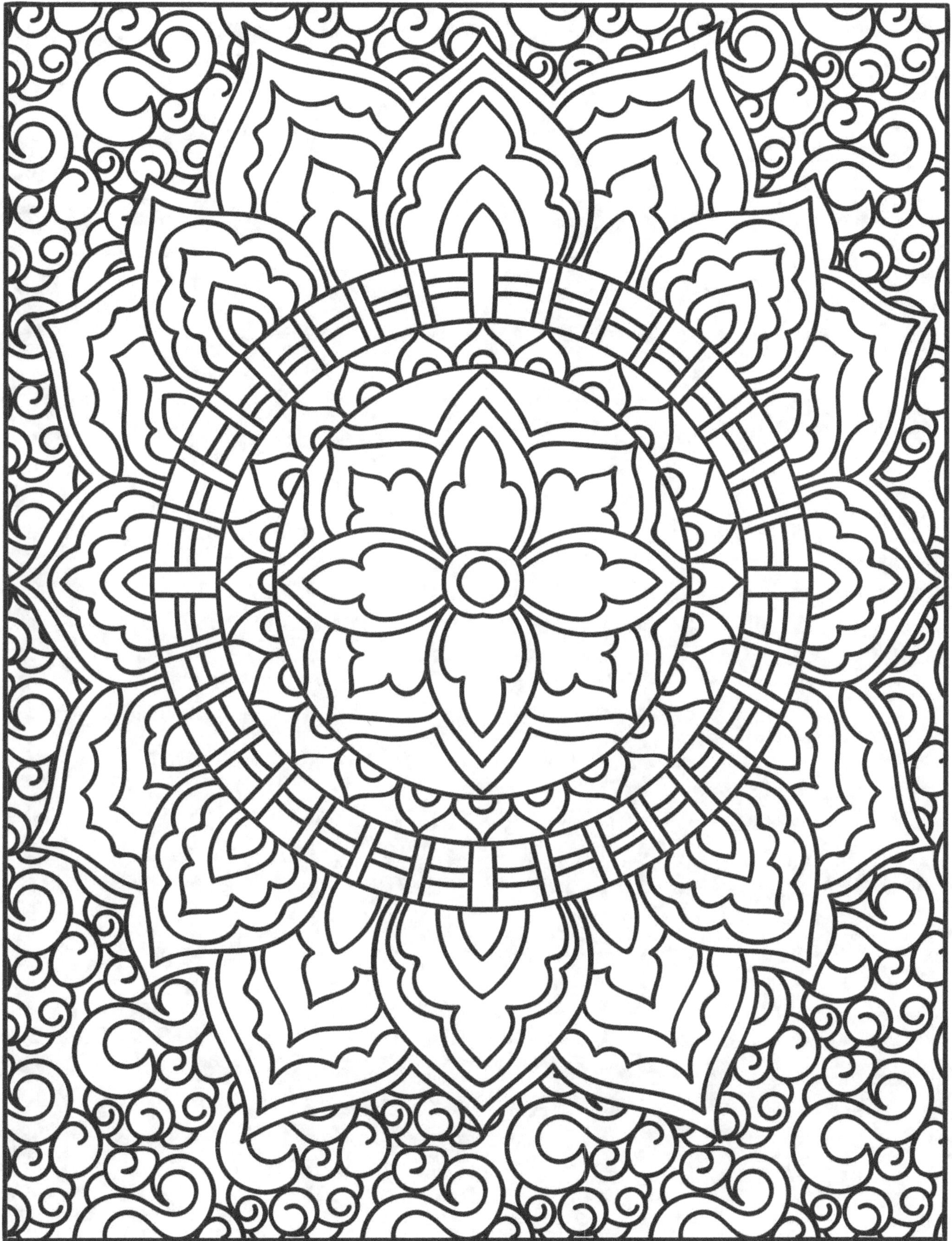

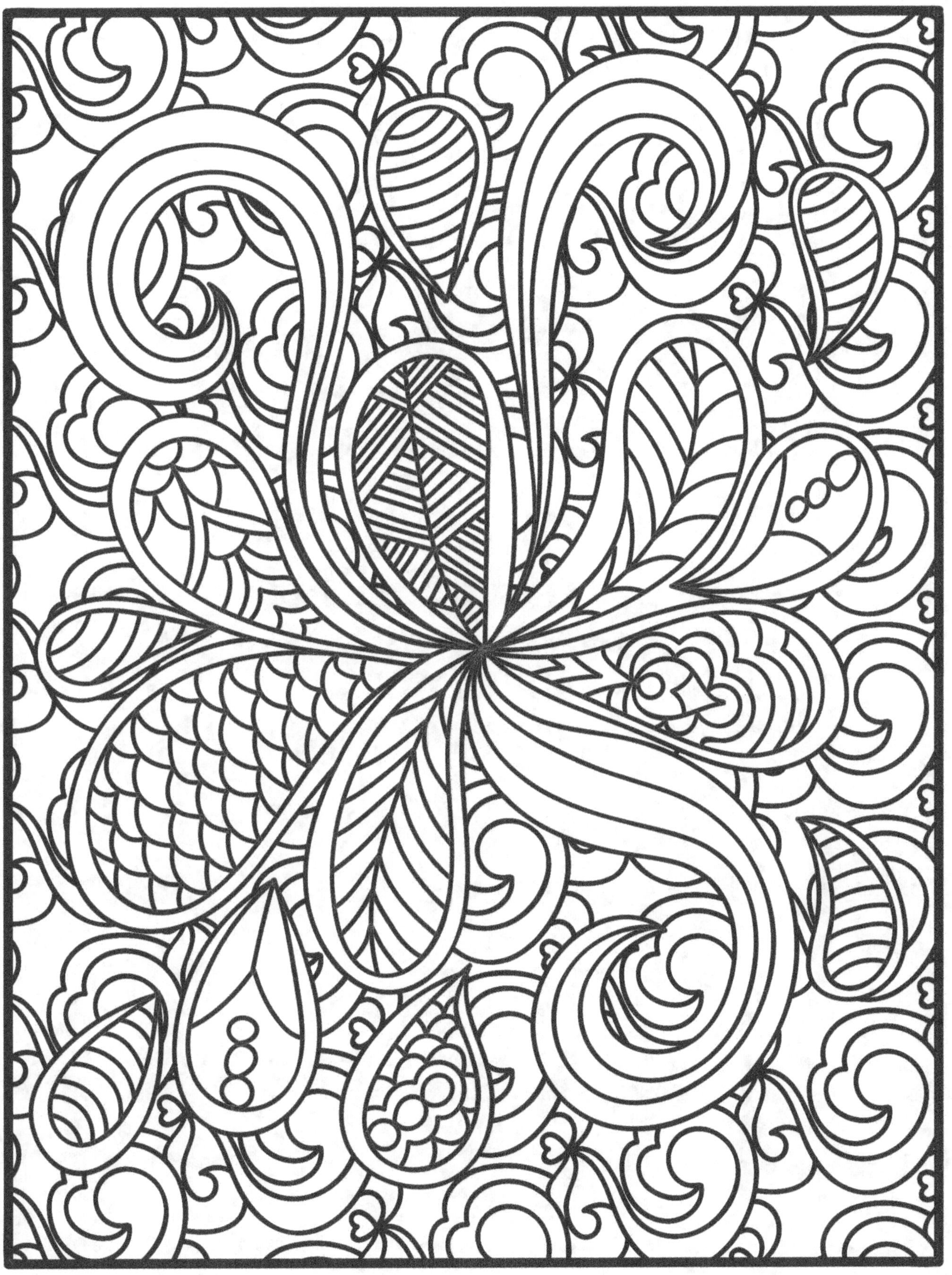

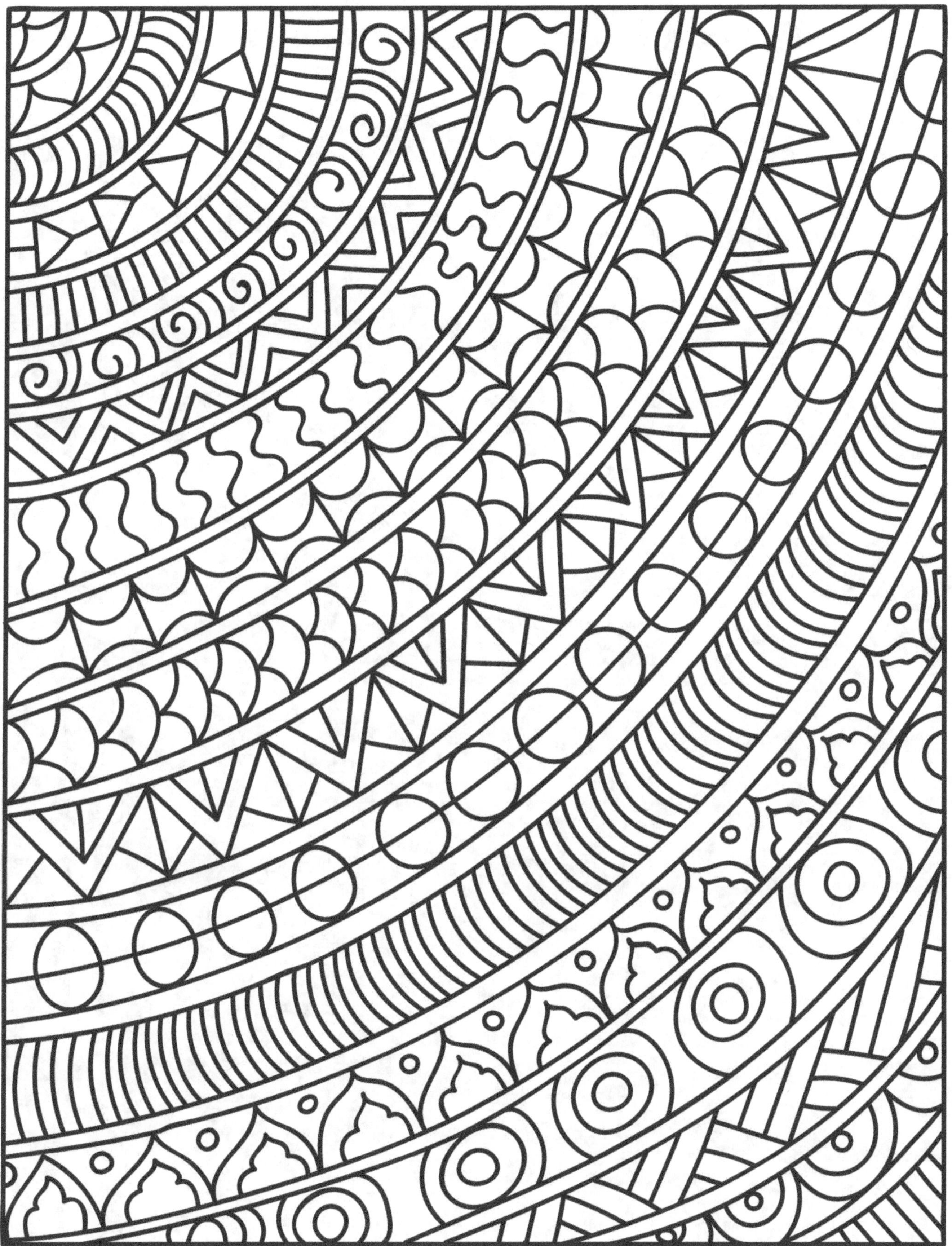

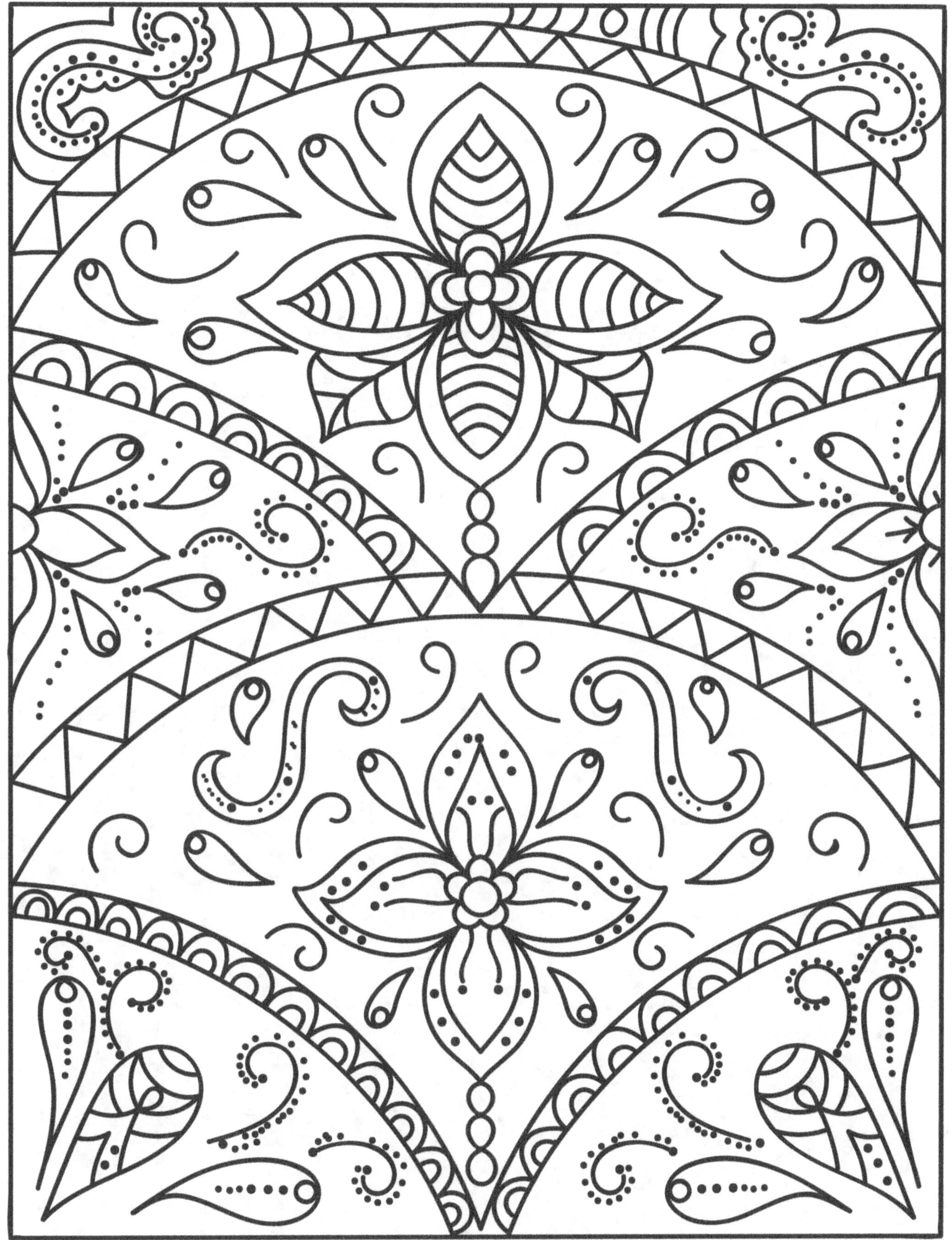

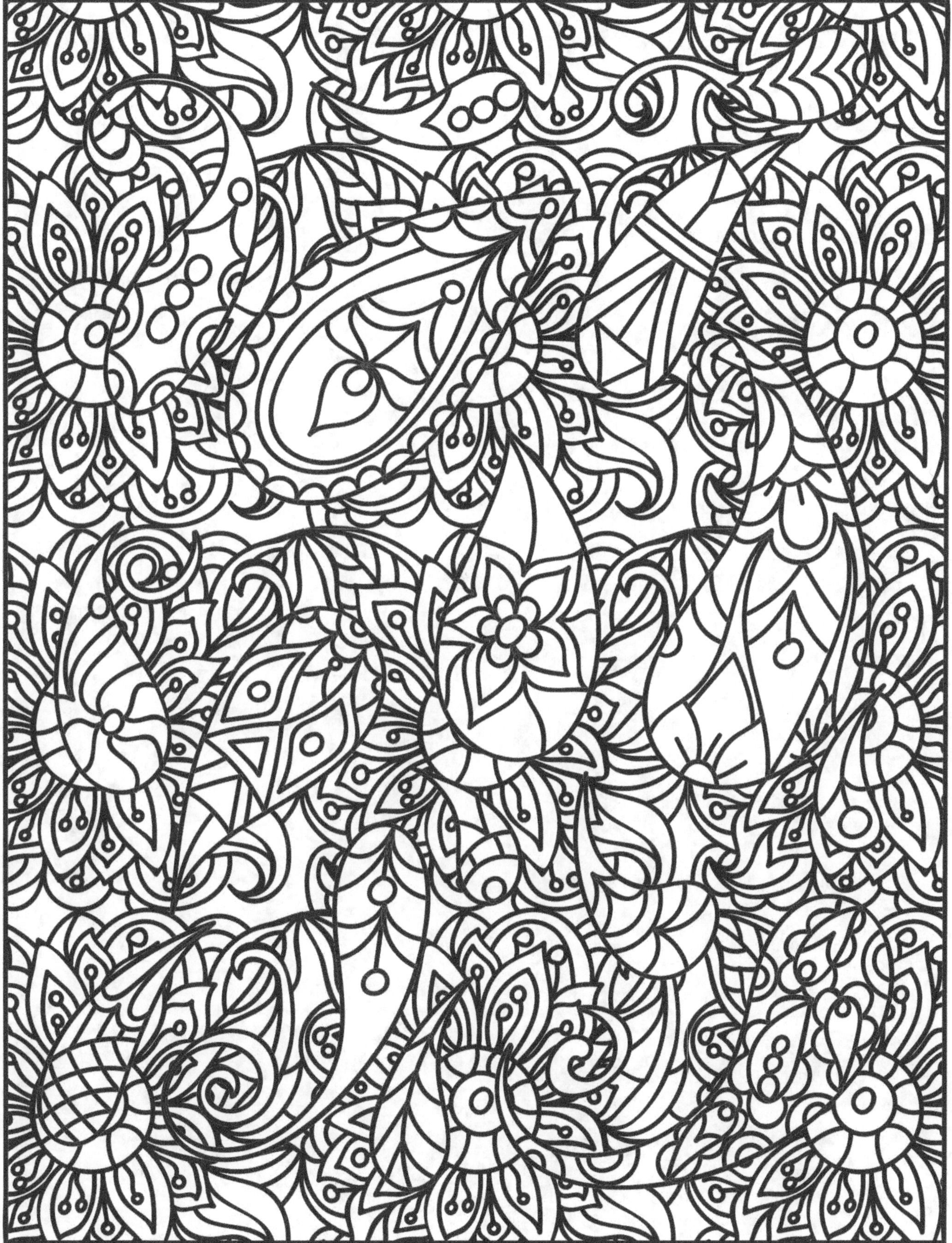

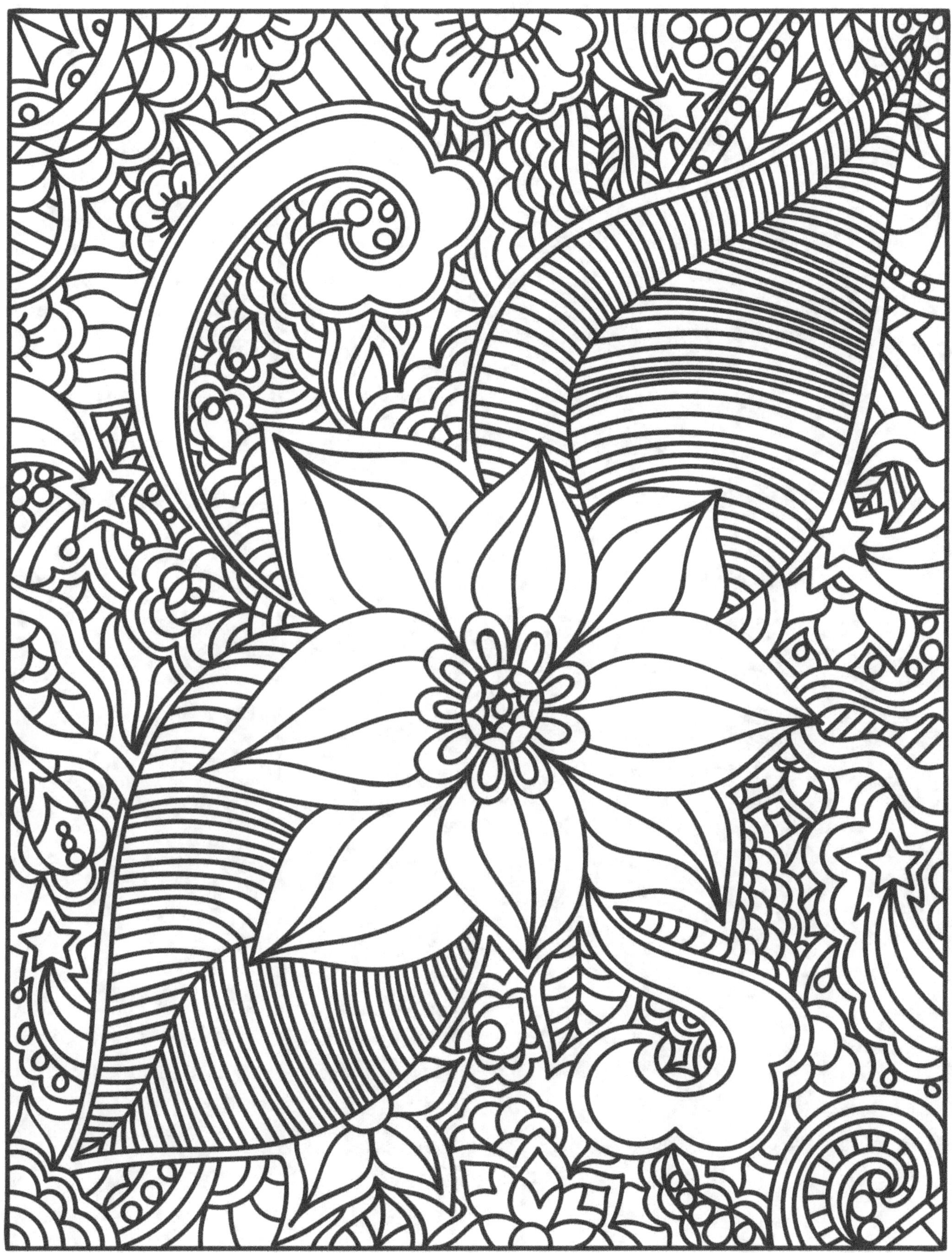

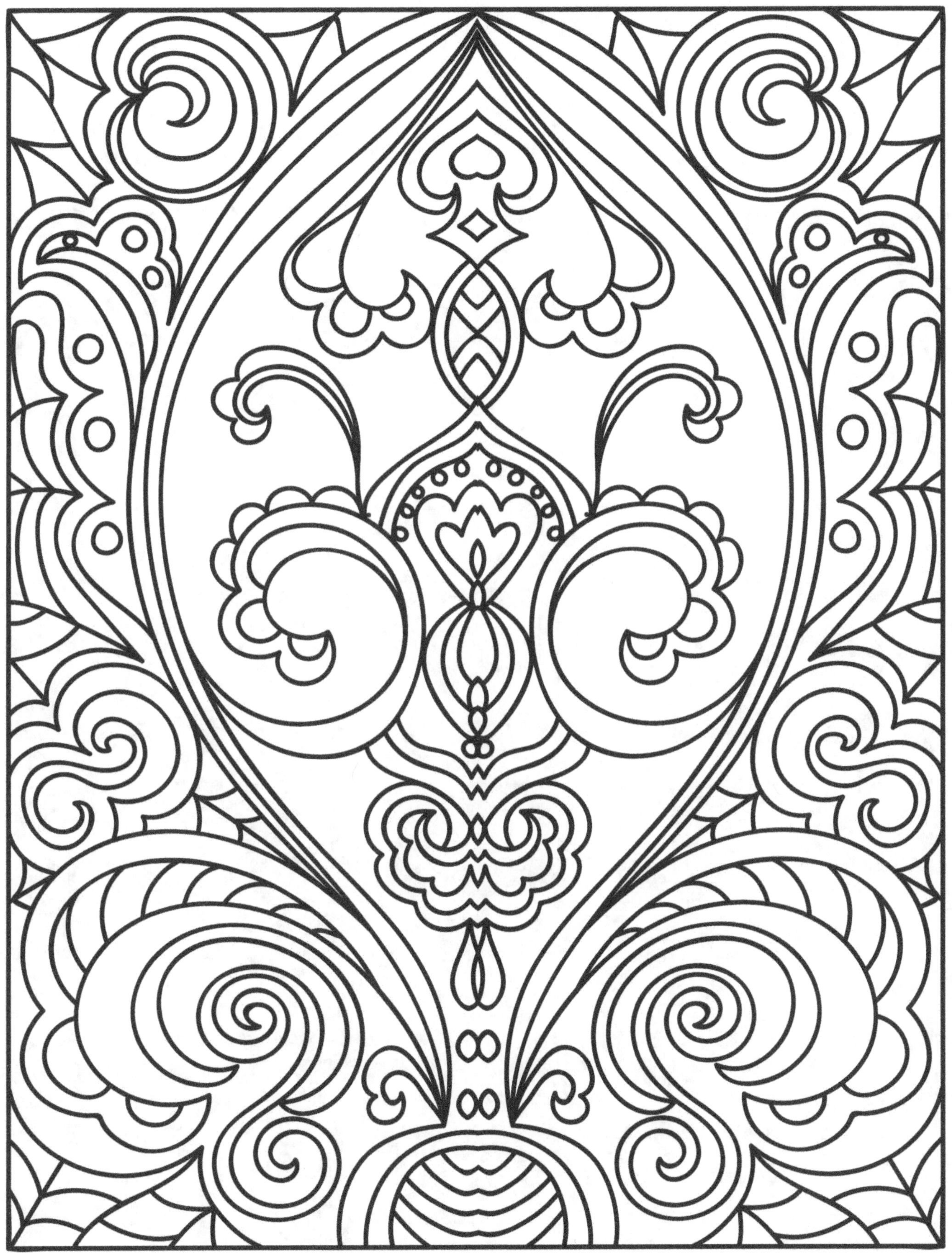

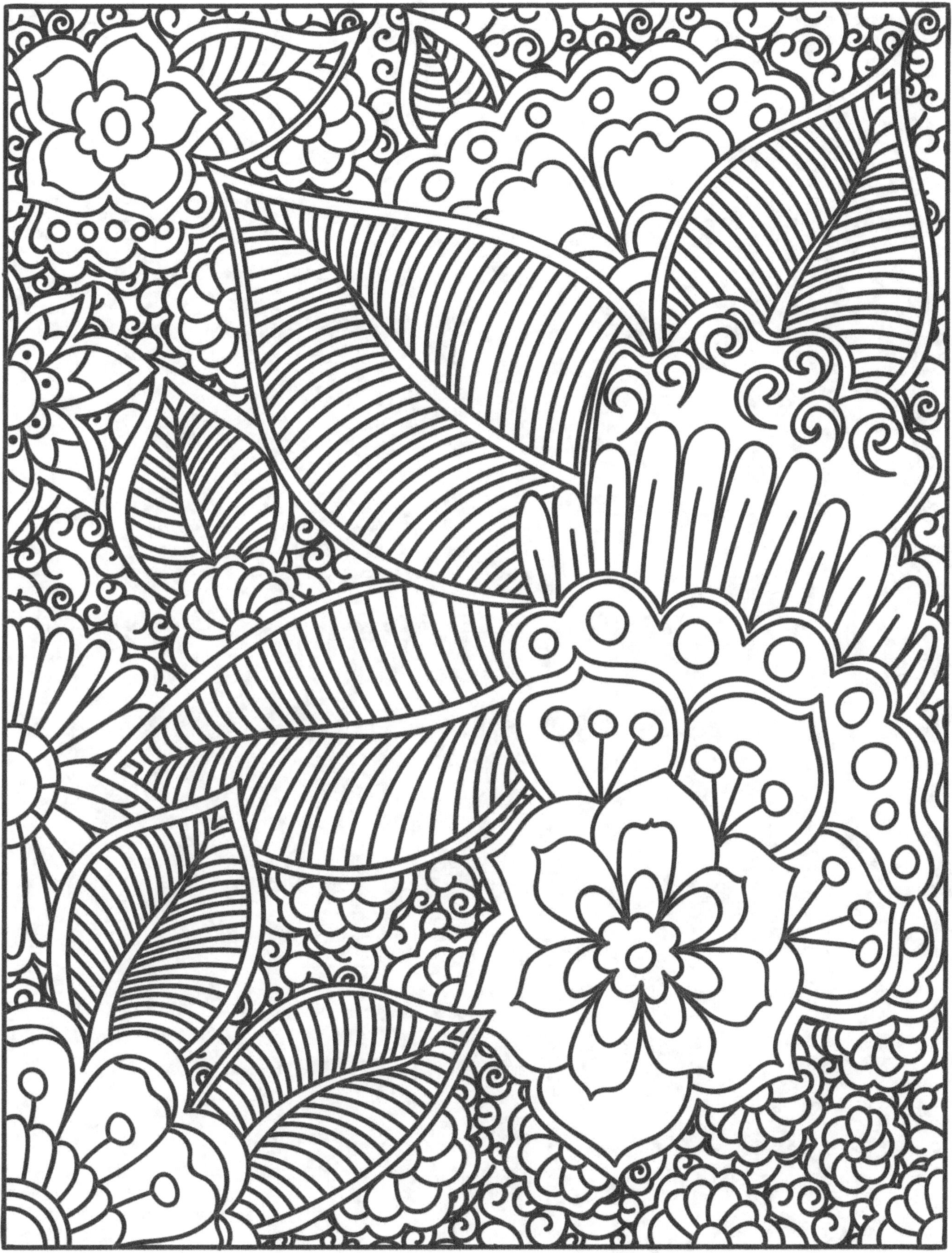

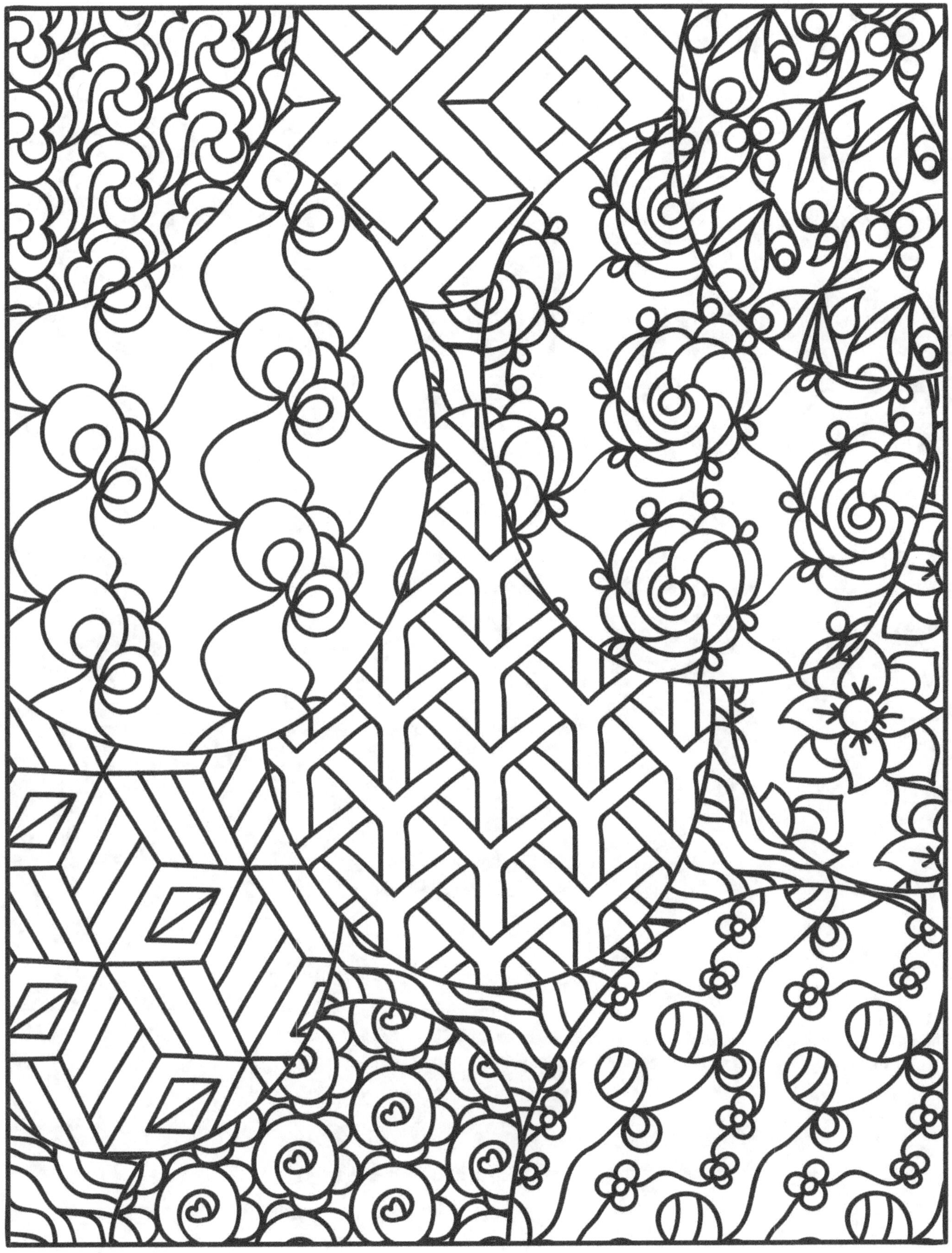

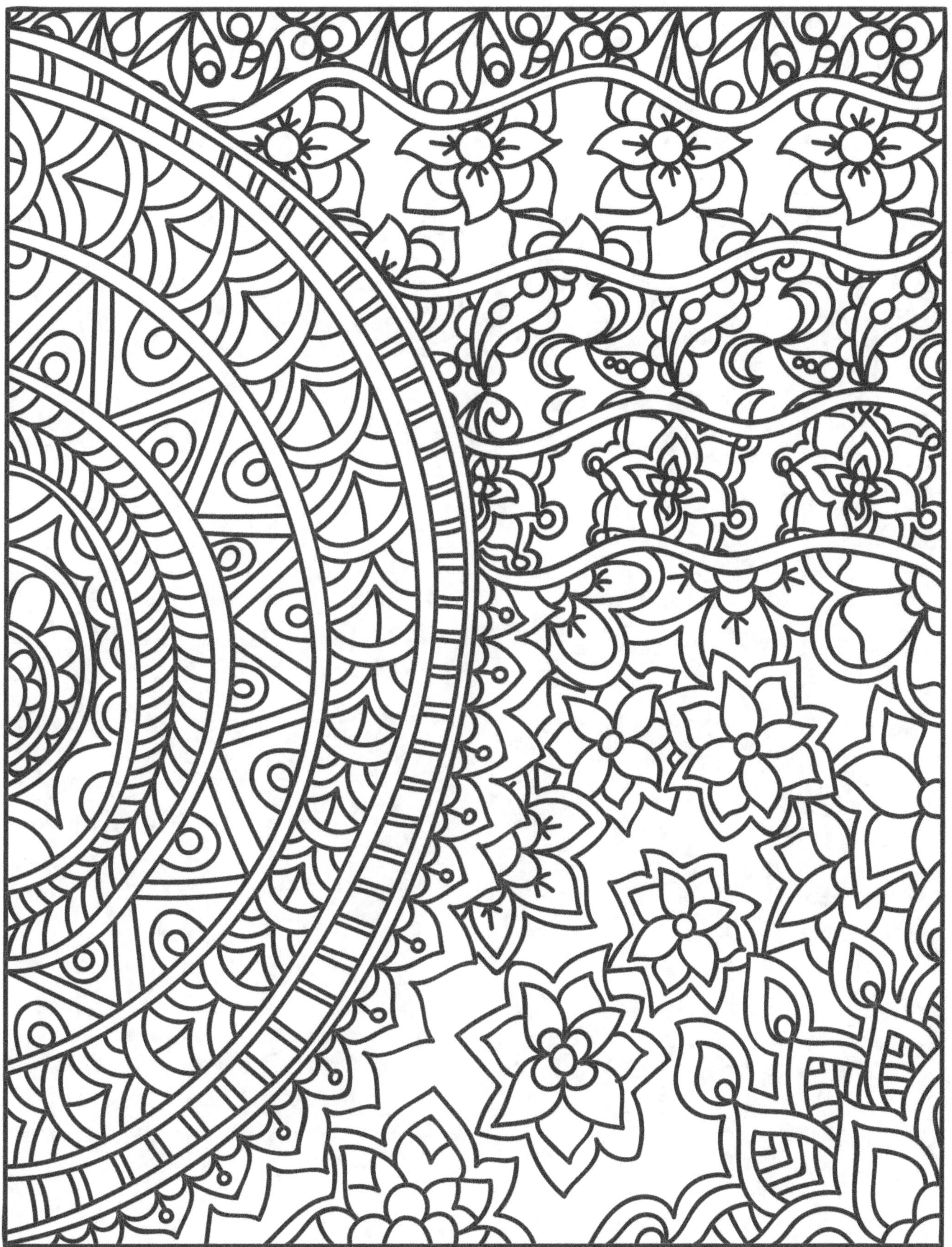

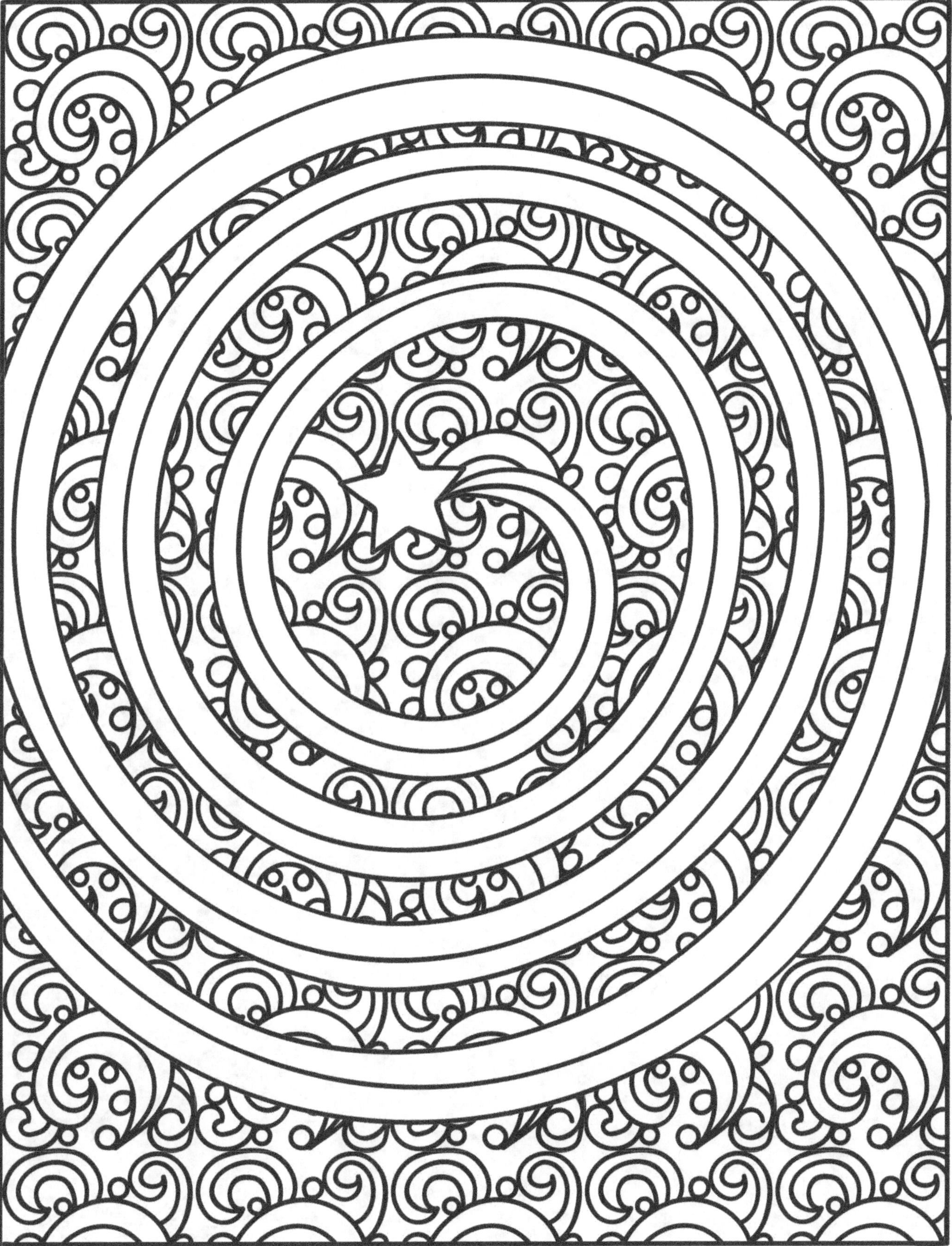

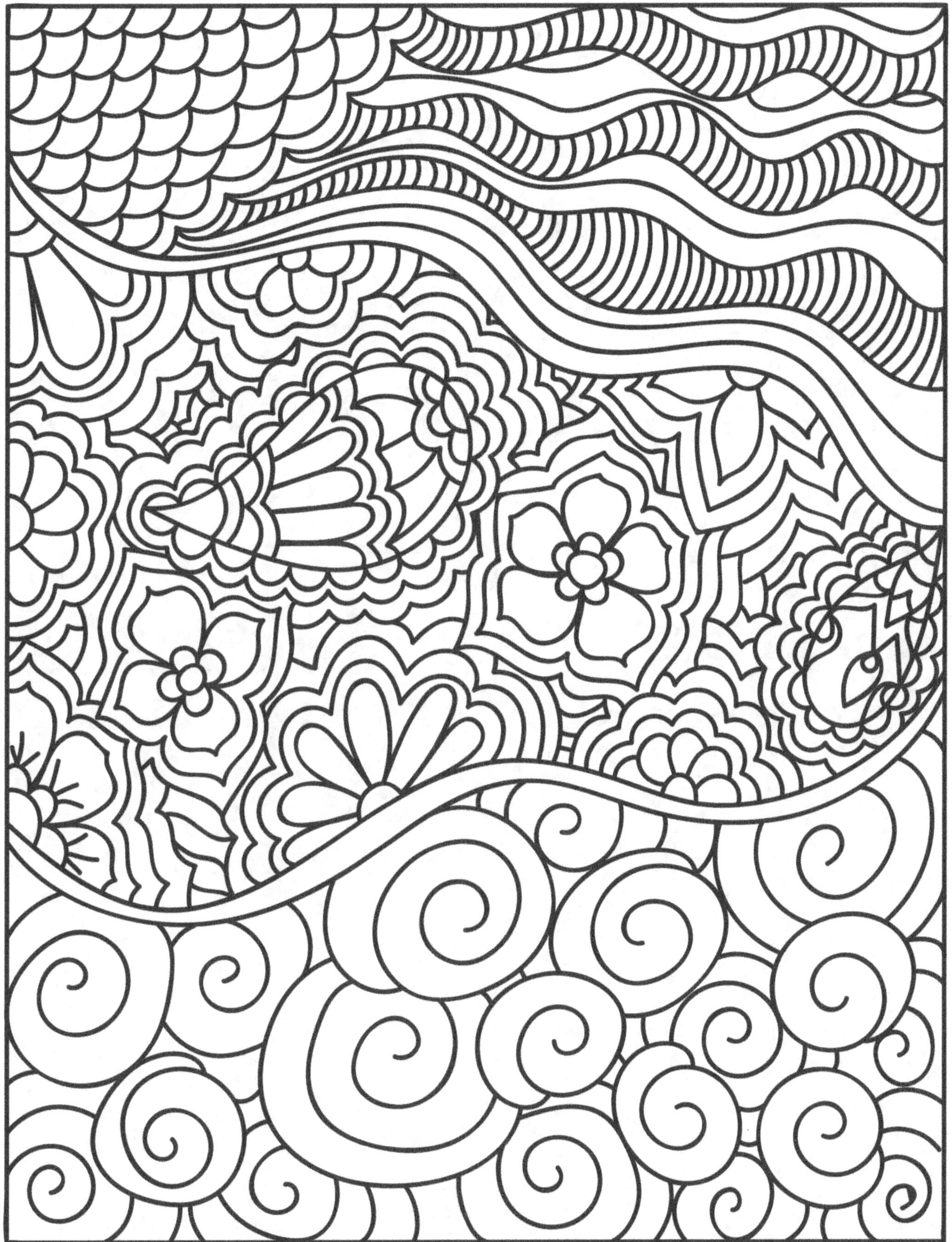

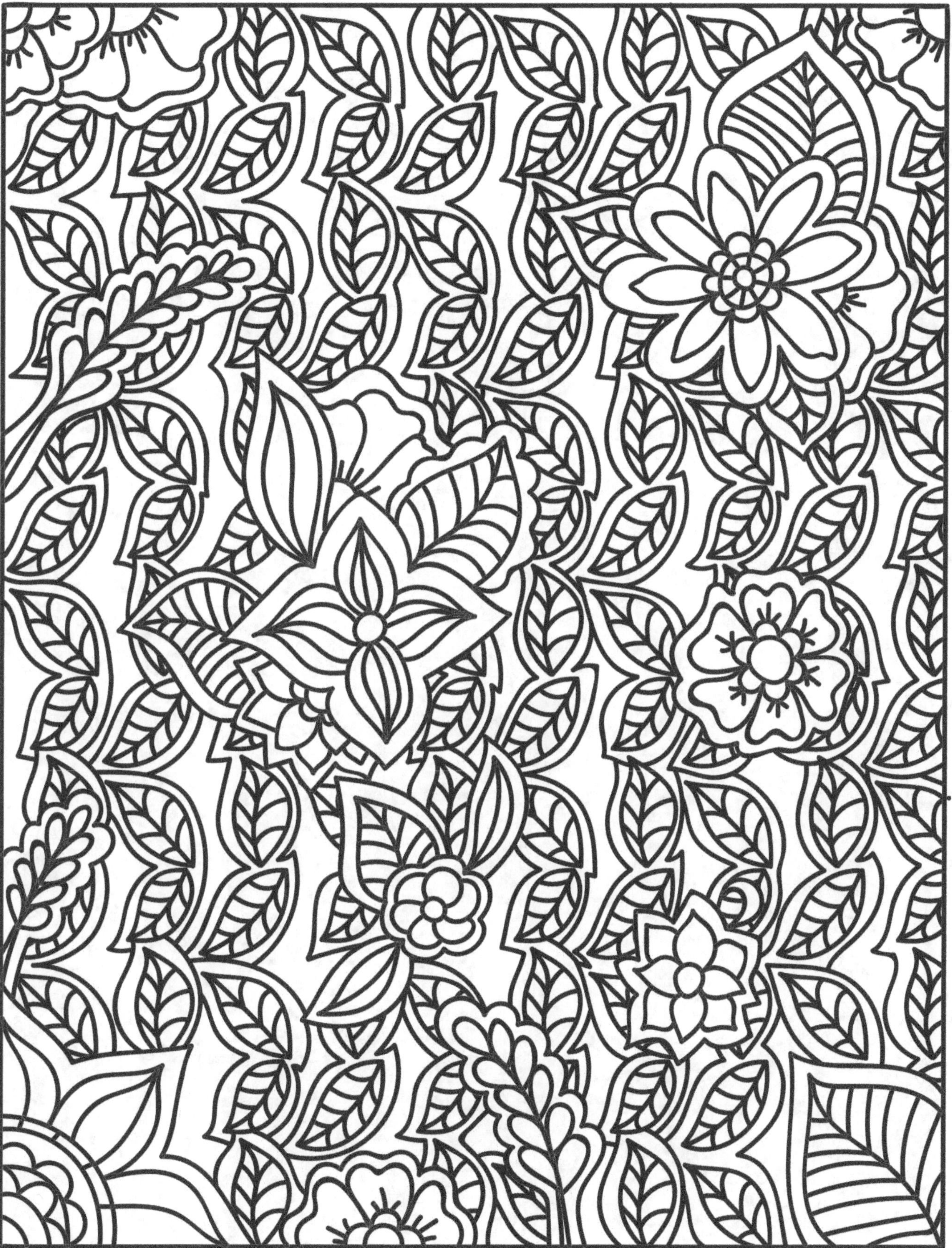

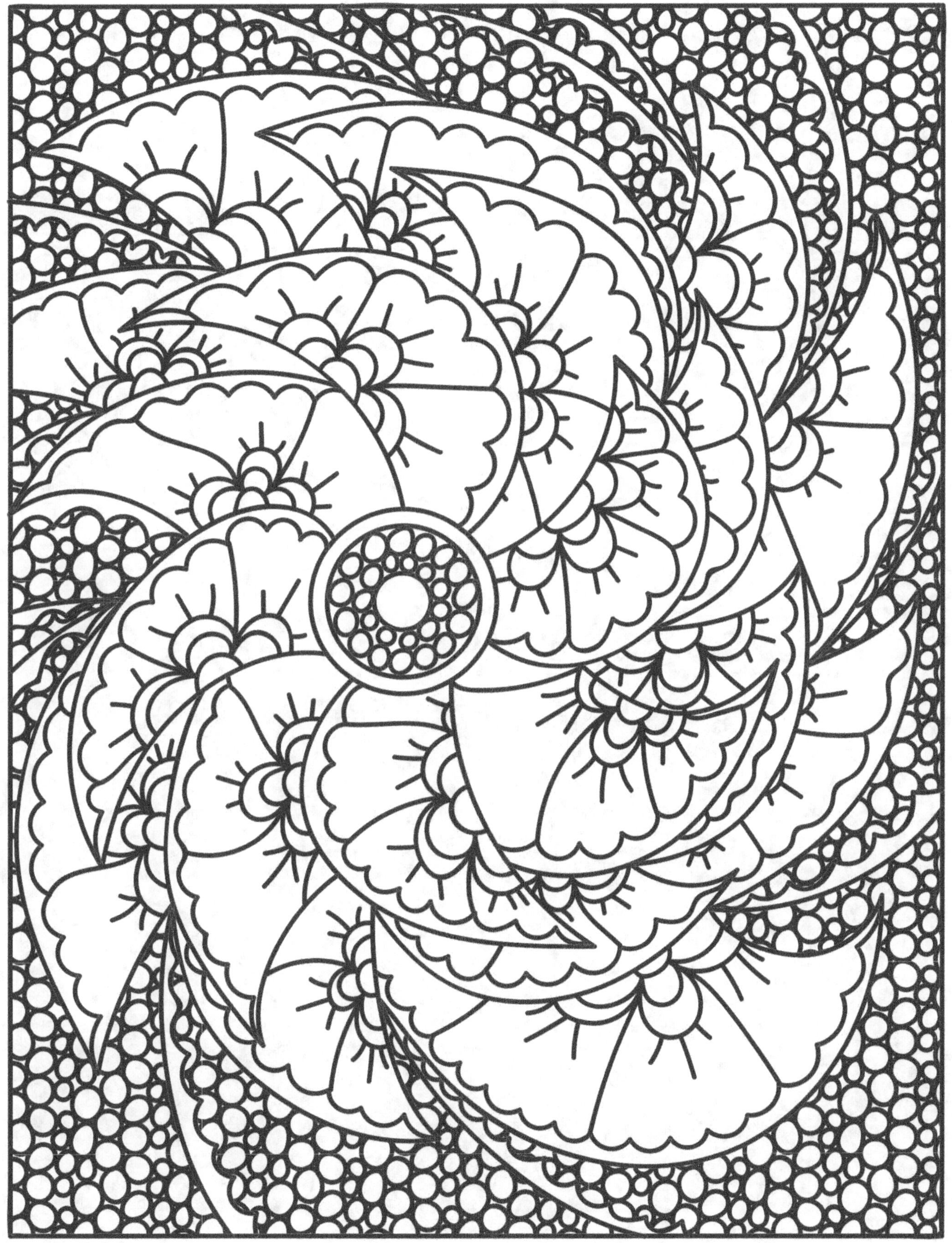

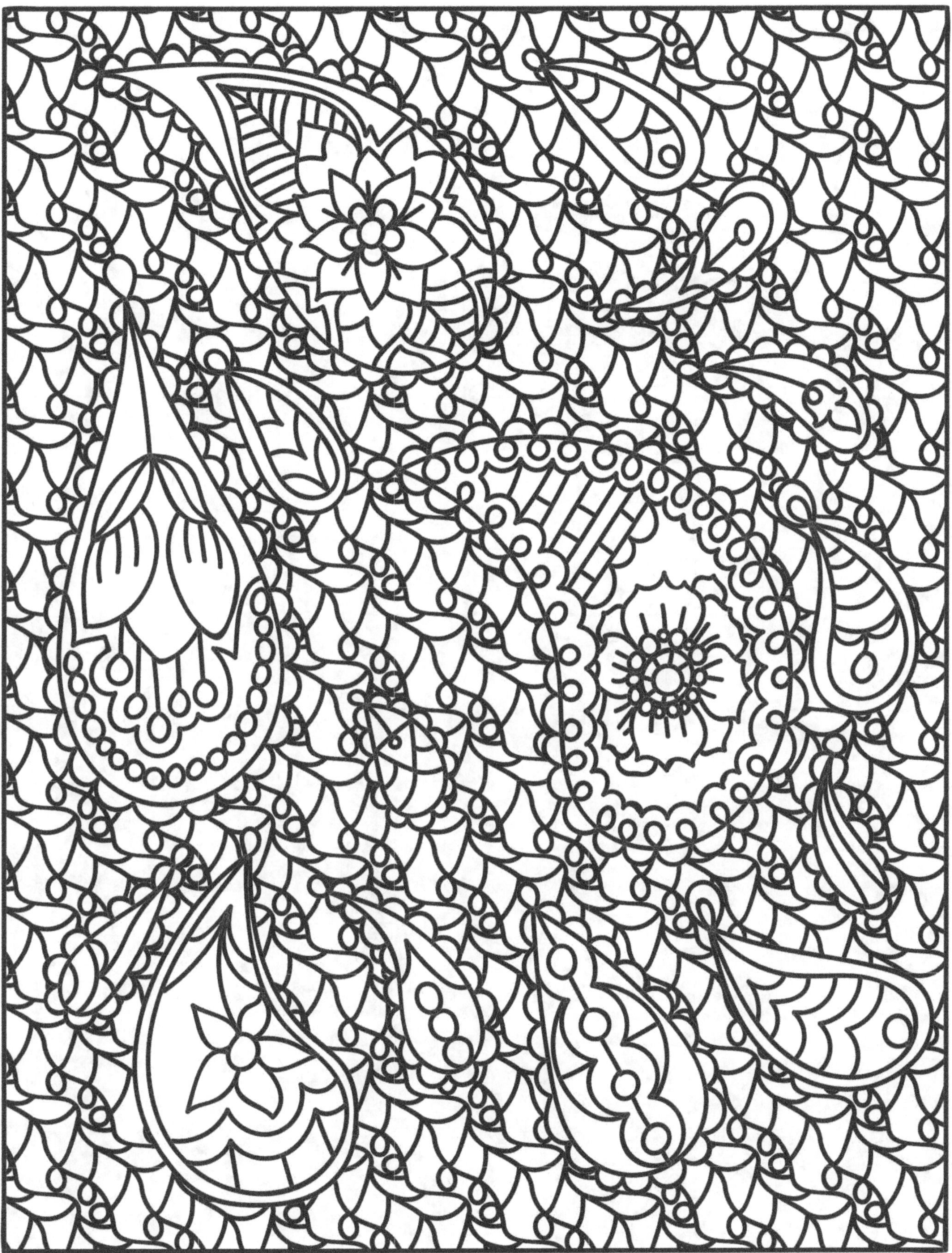

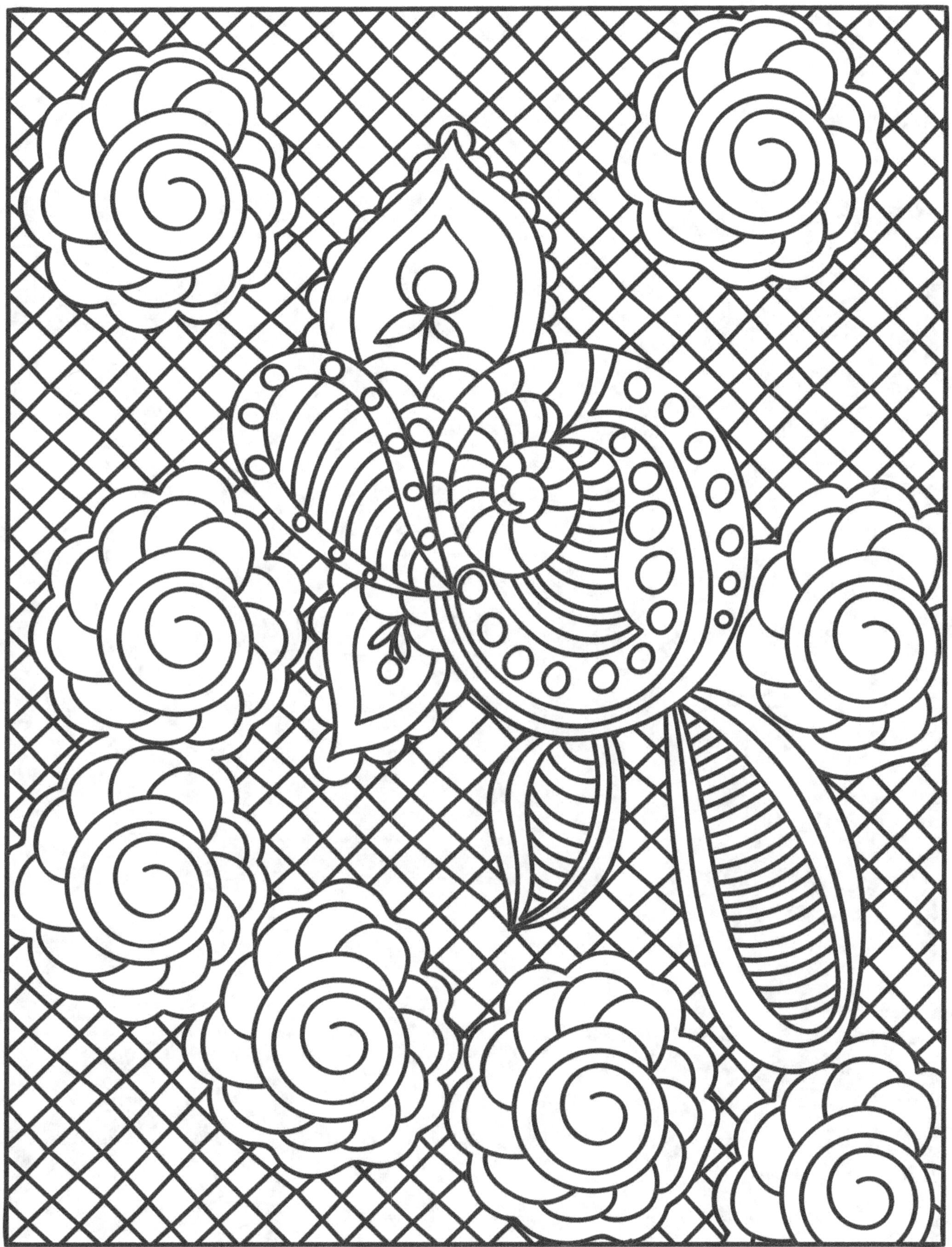

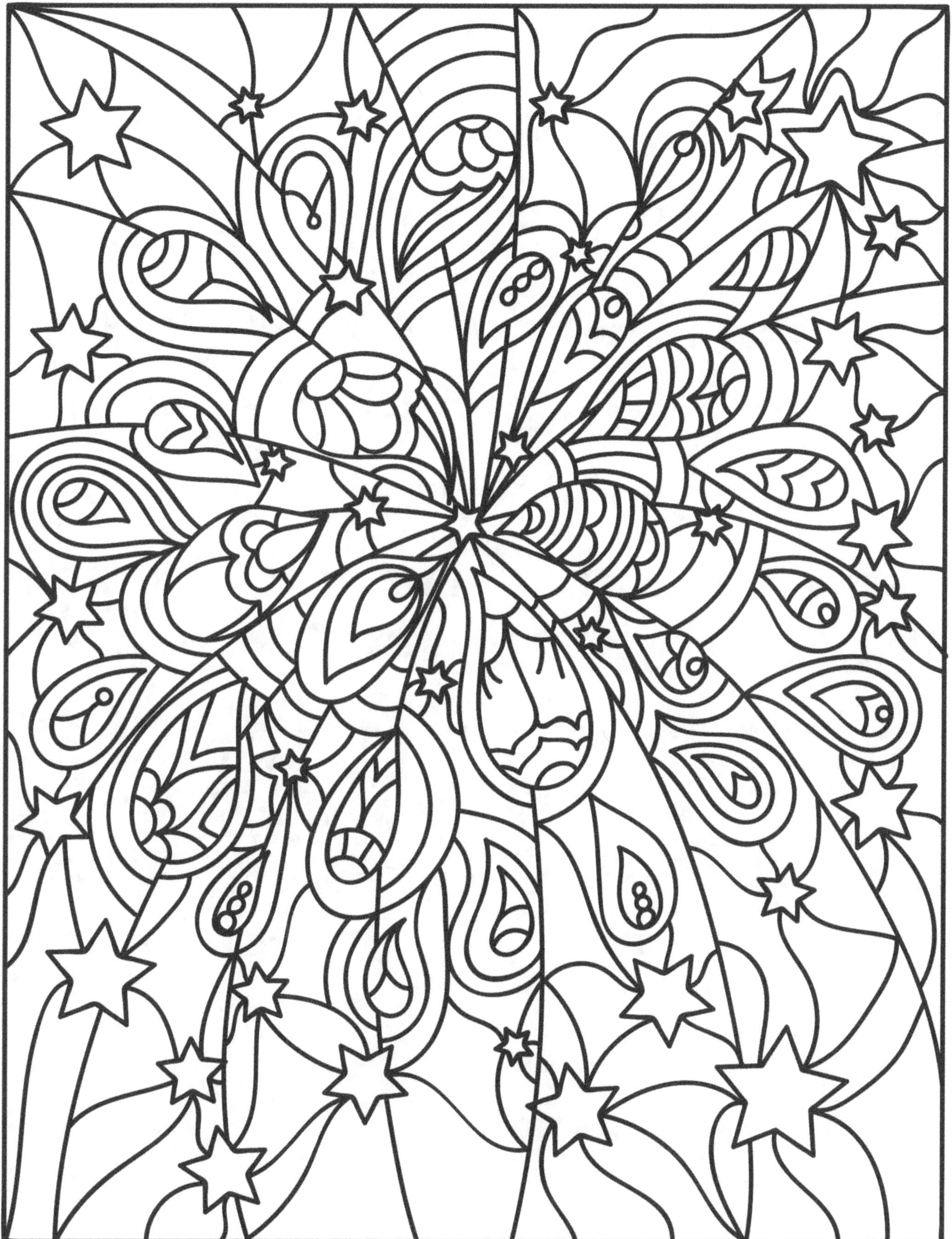

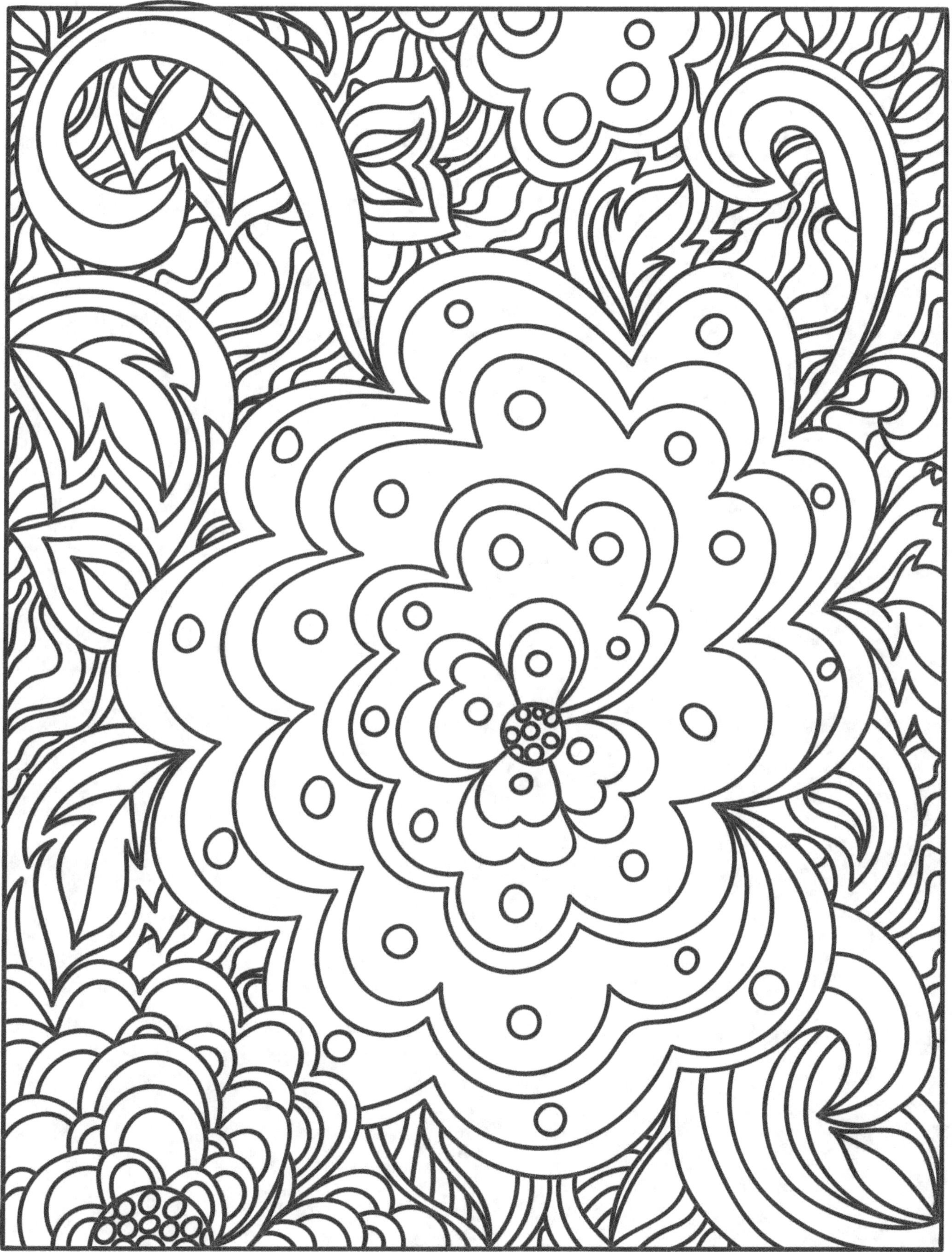

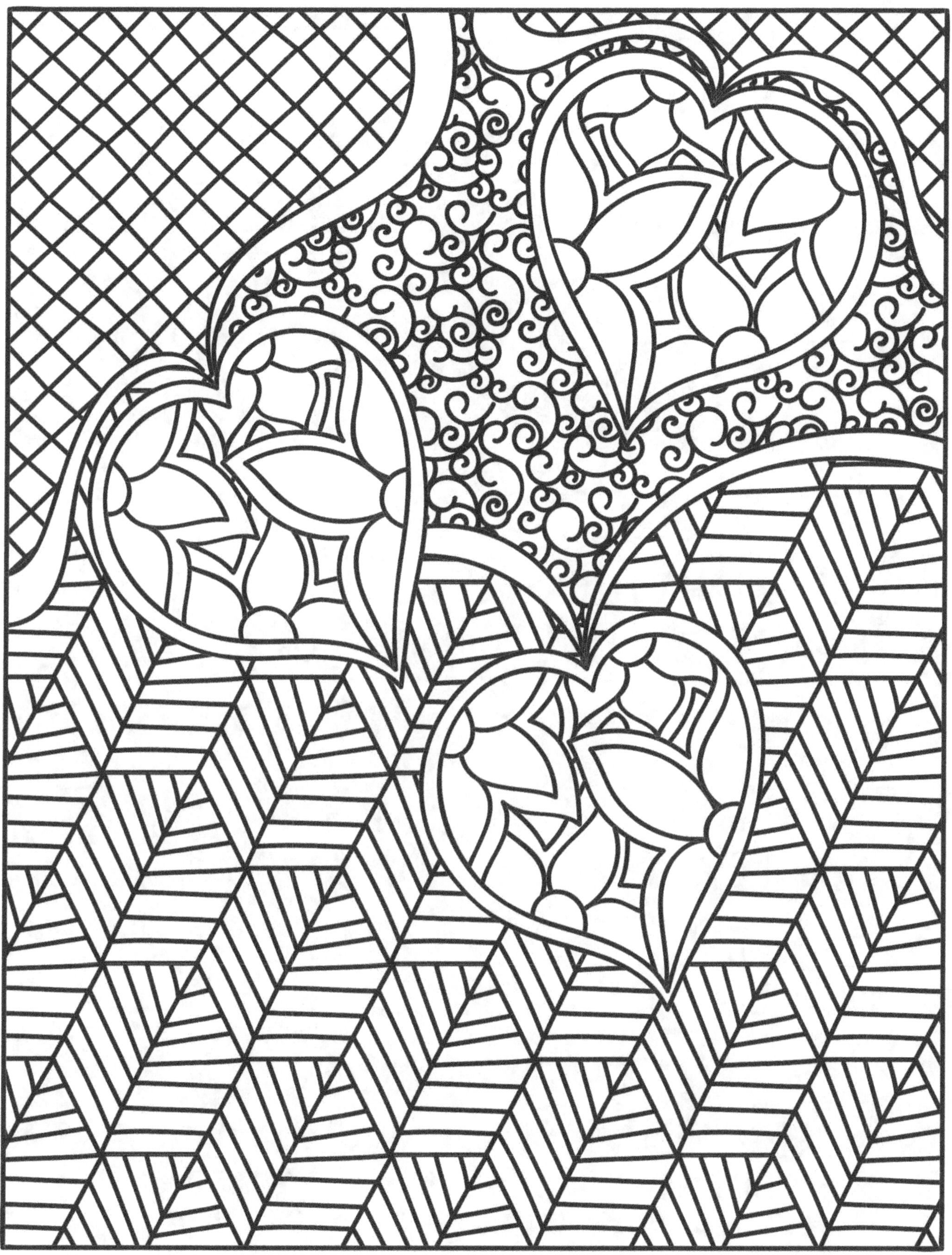

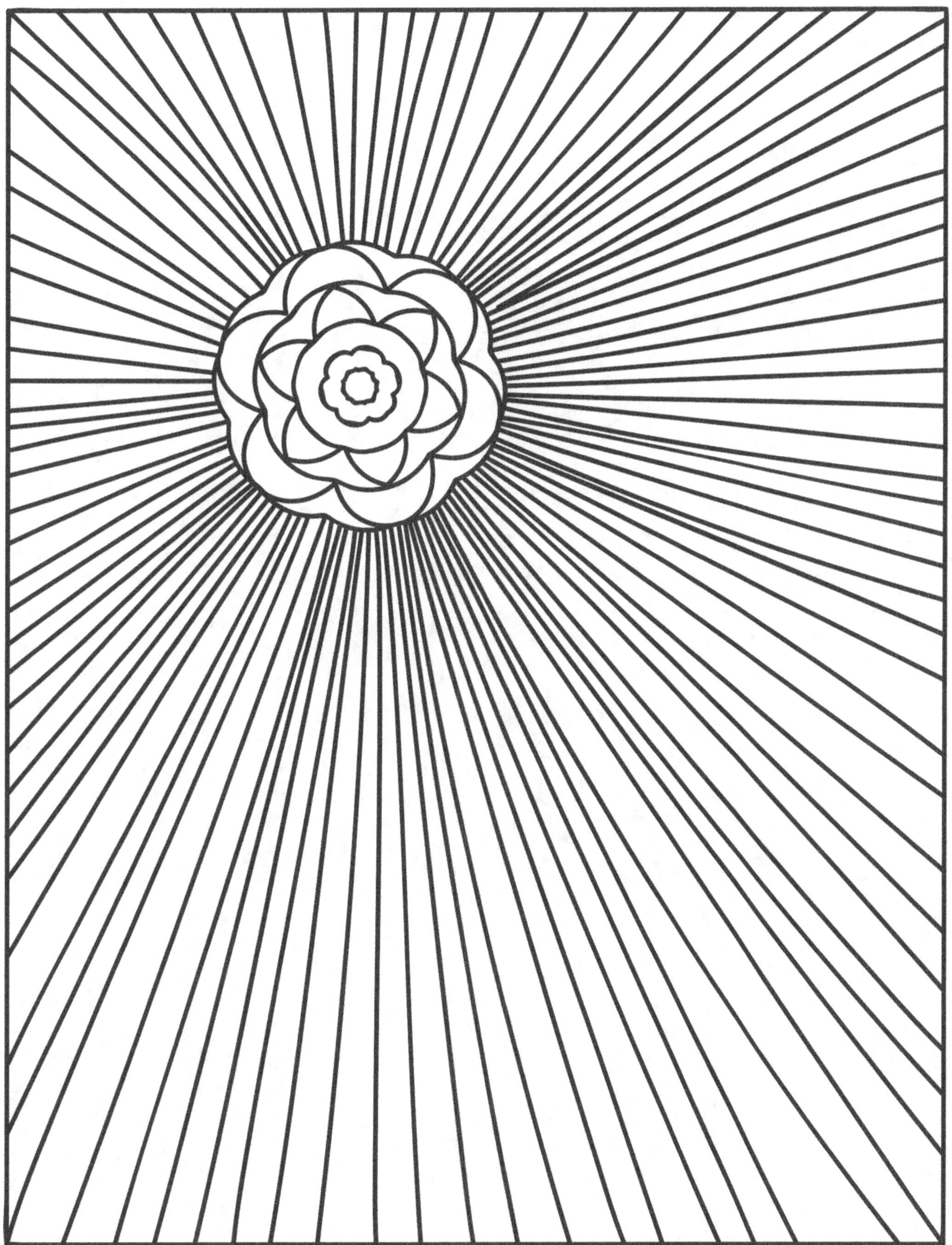

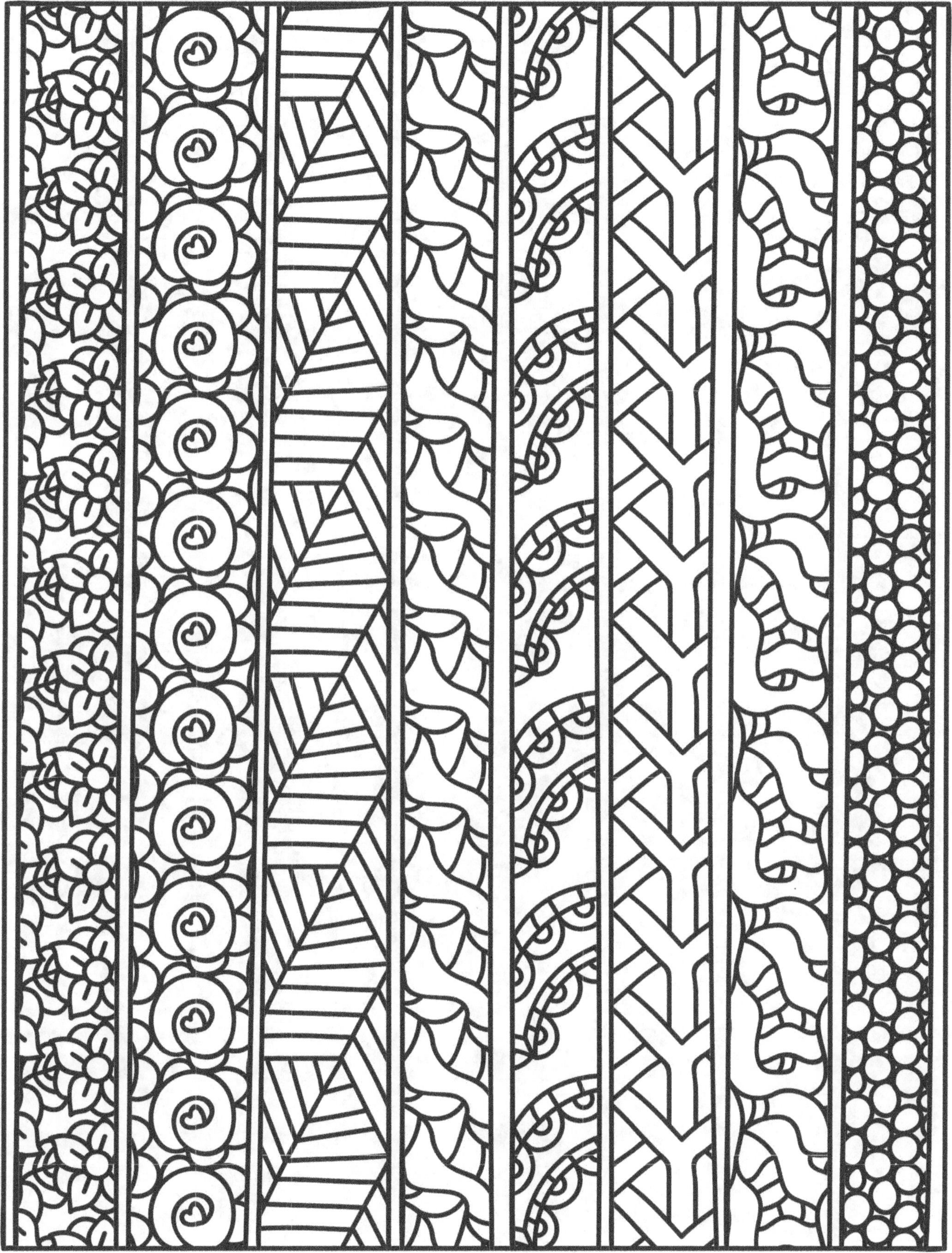

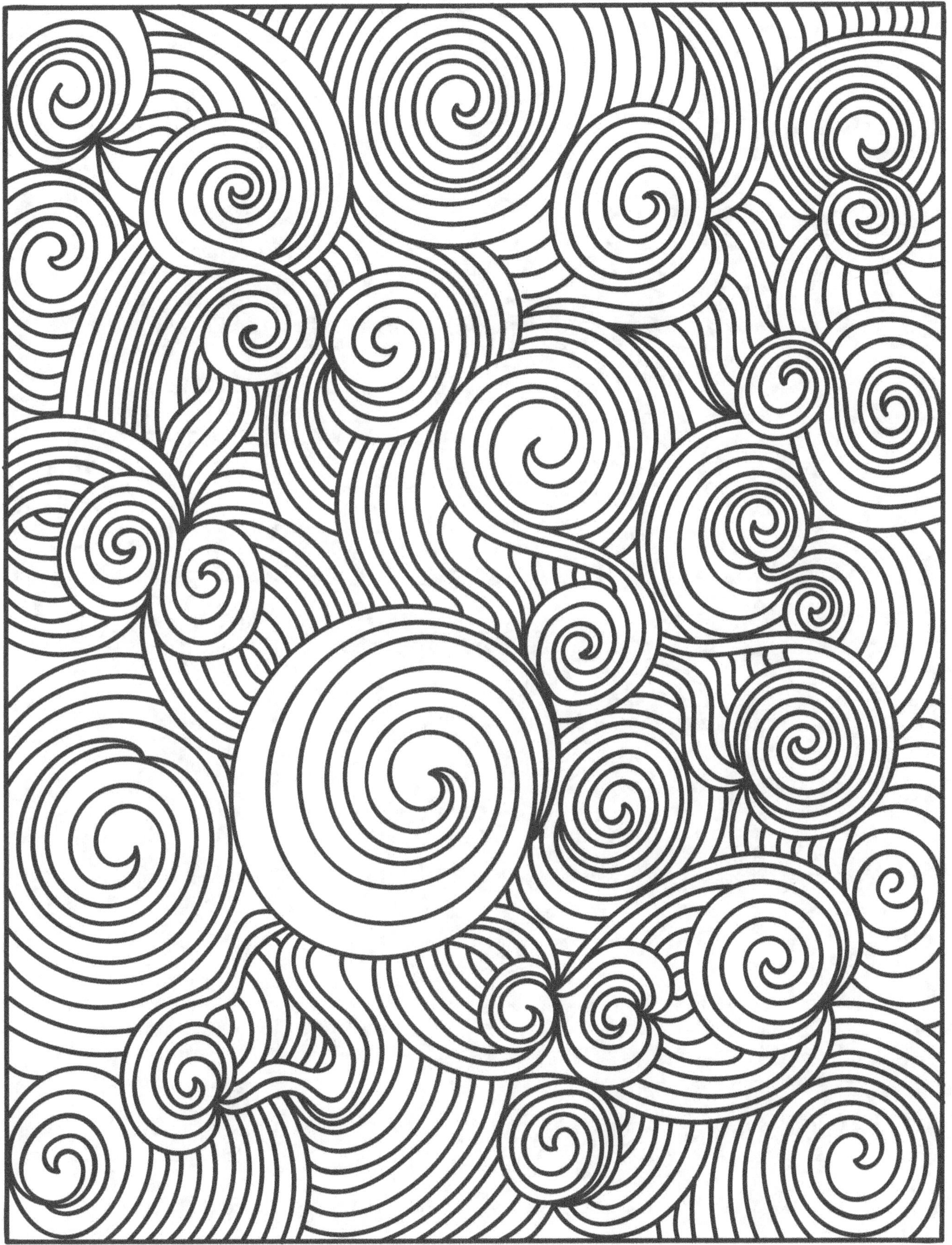

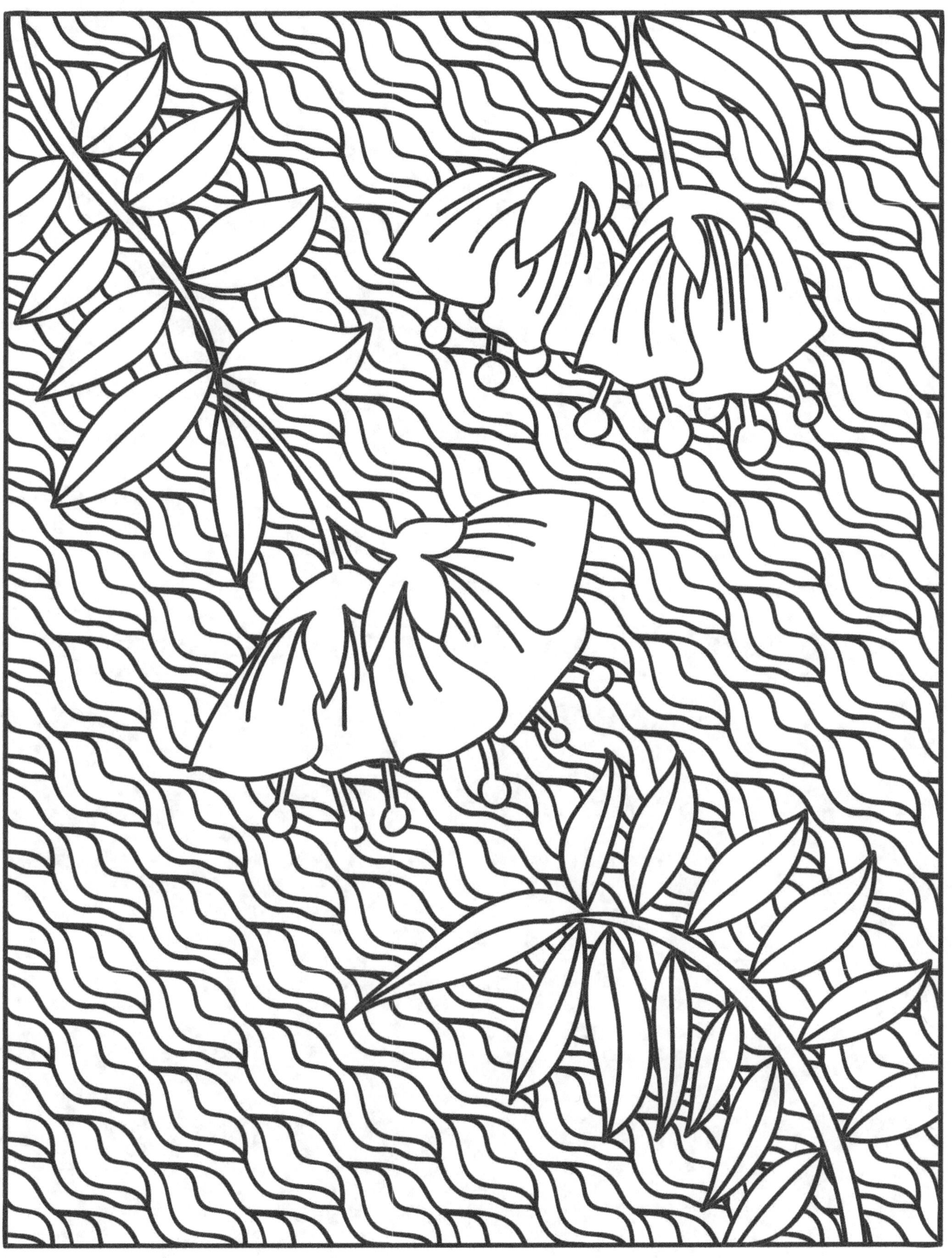

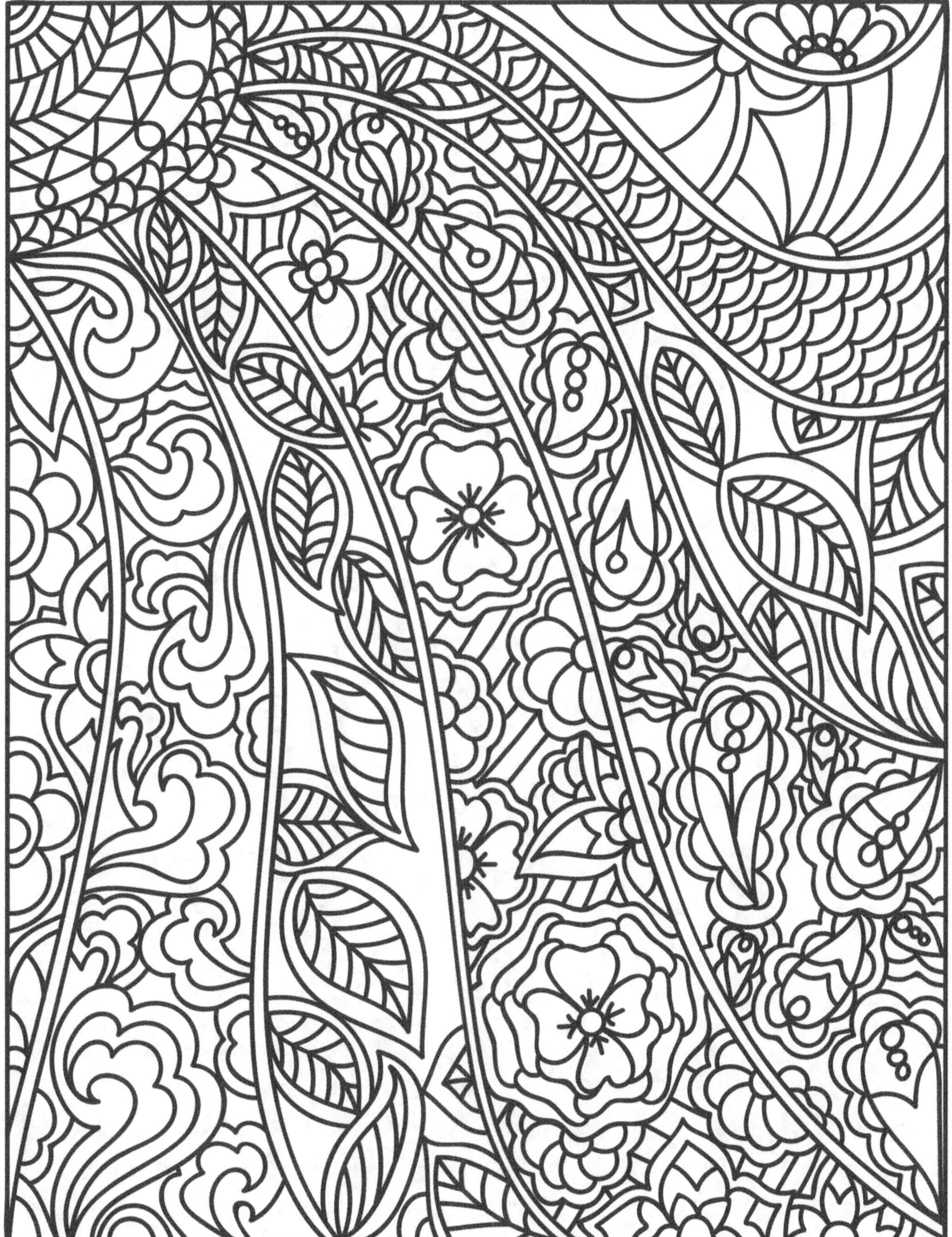

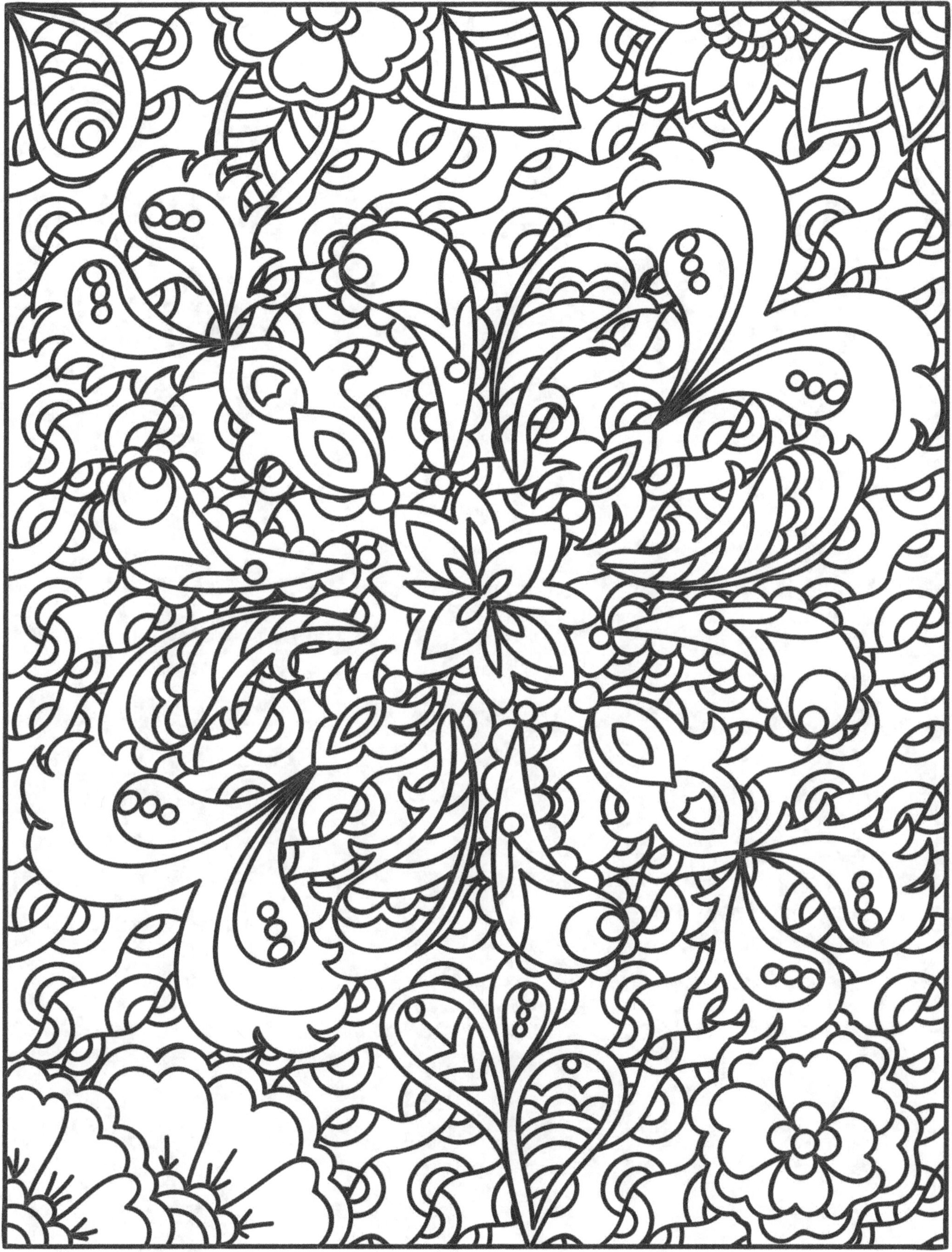

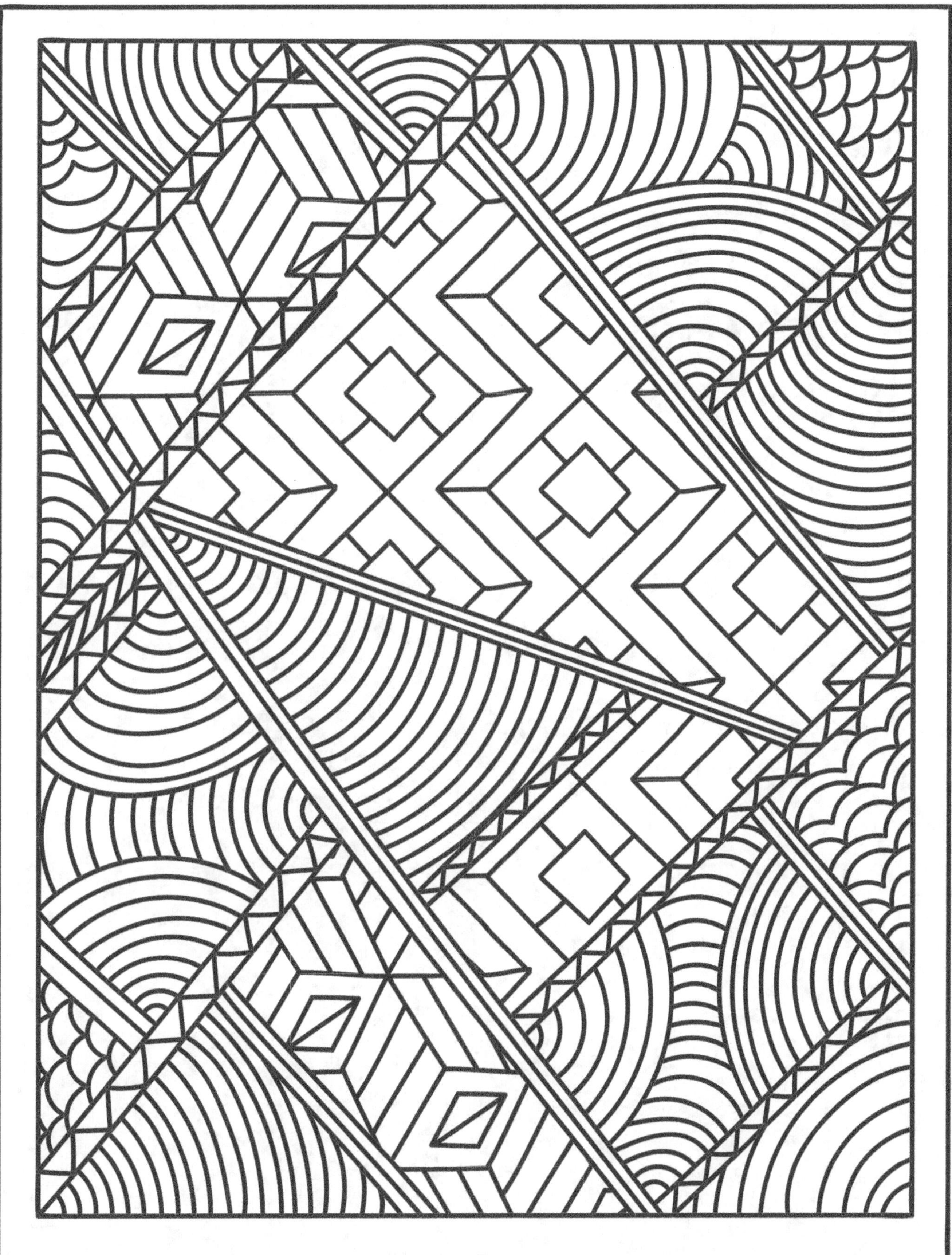

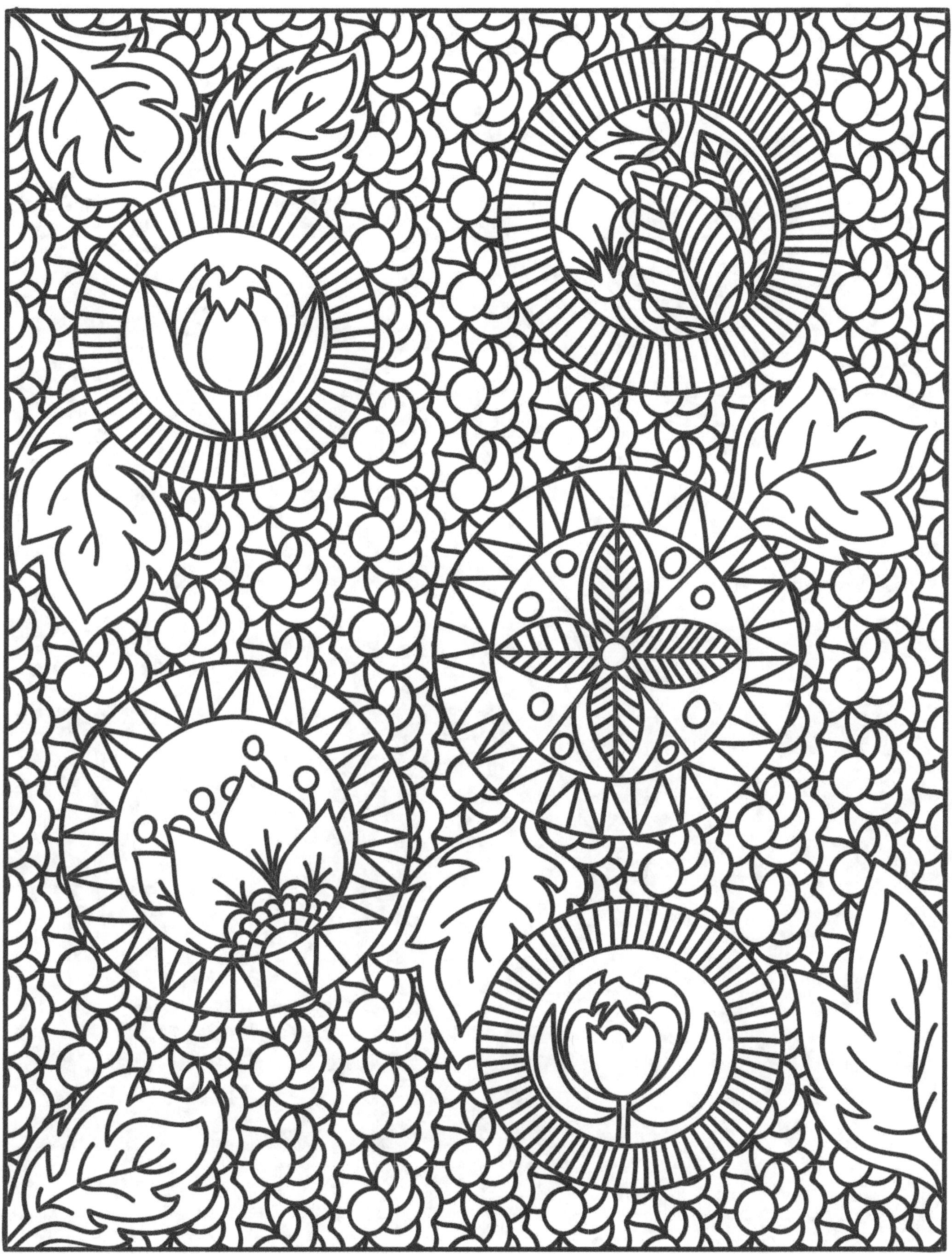

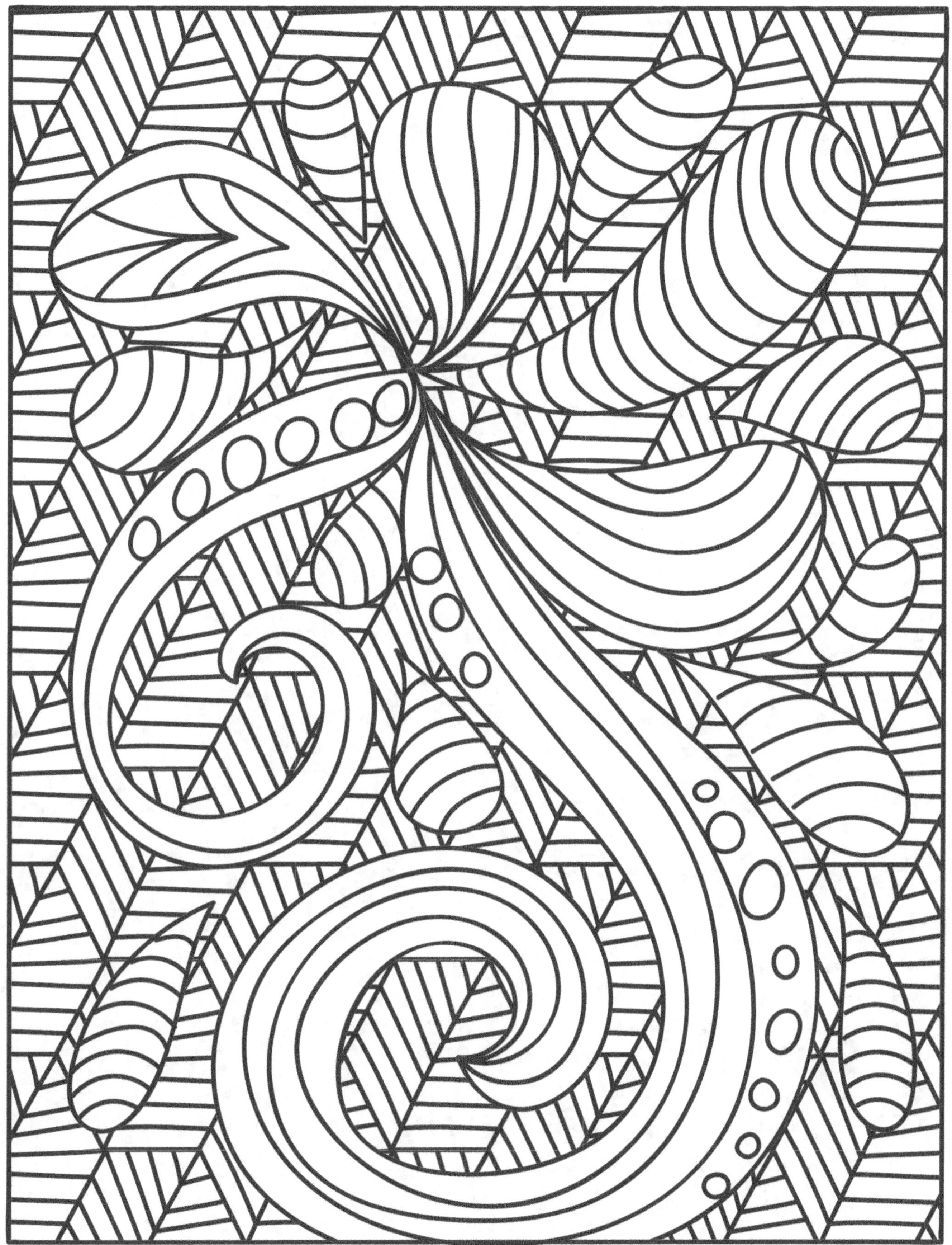

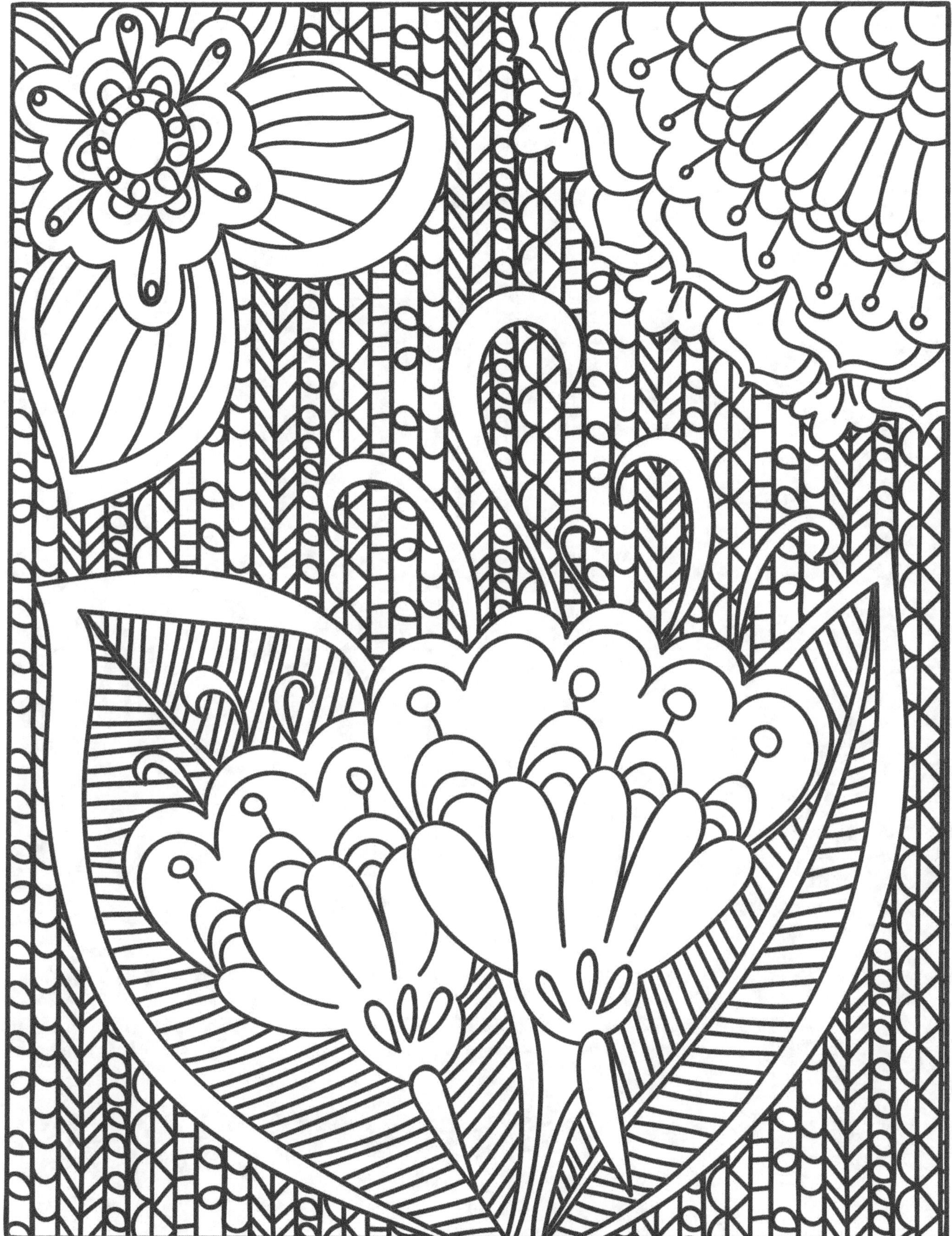

COLOR TEST PAGE

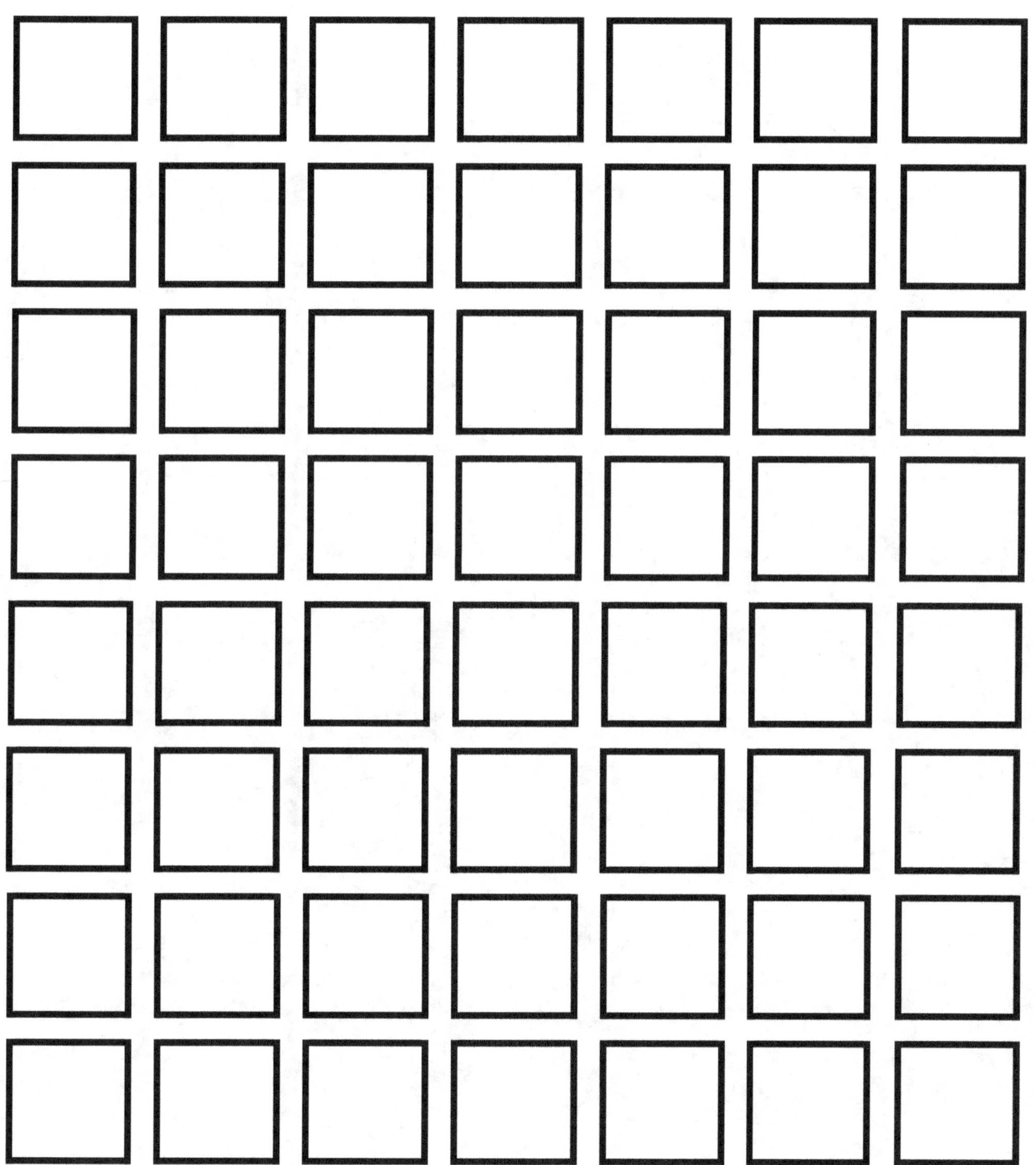

COLOR TEST PAGE

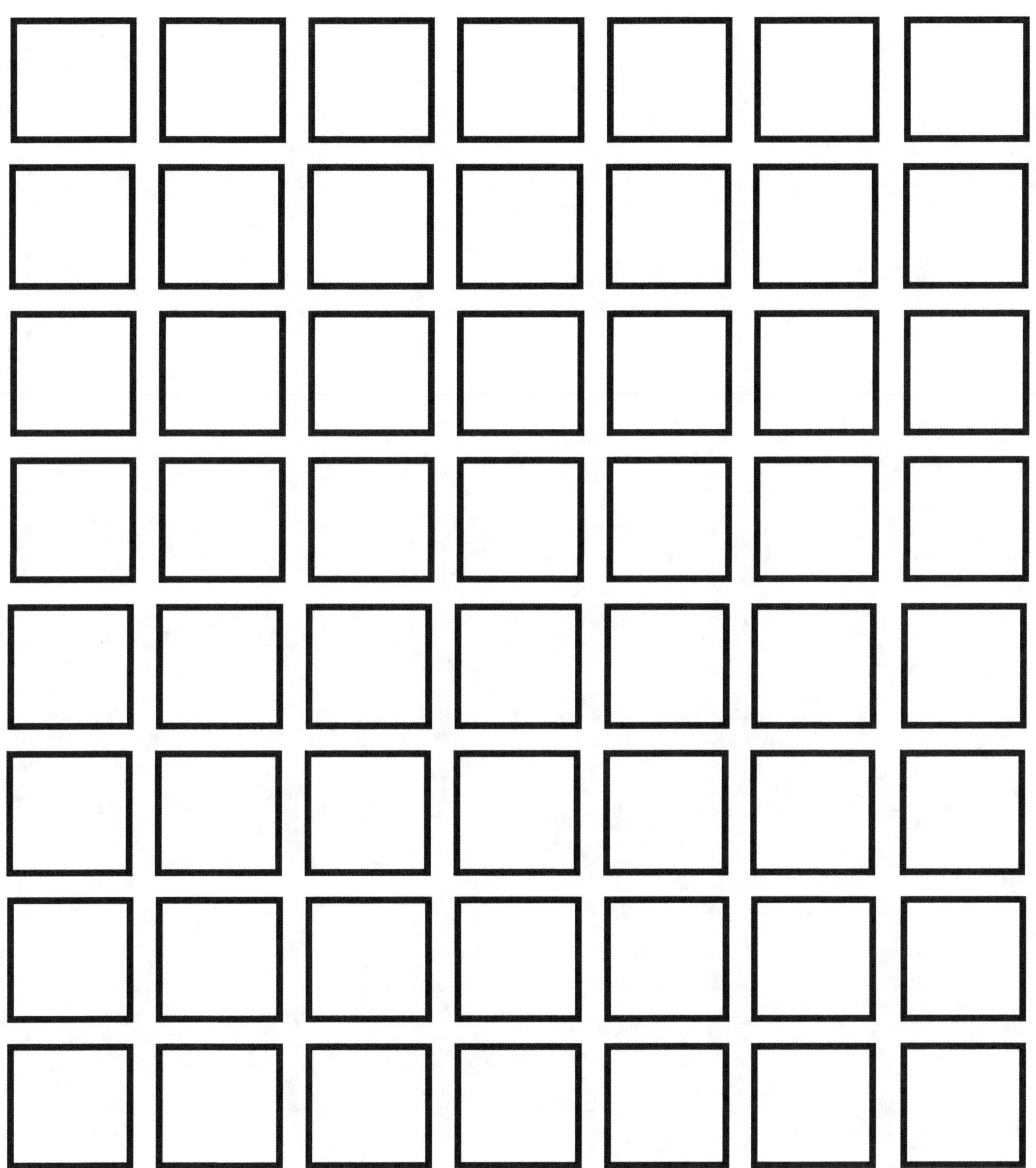

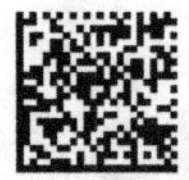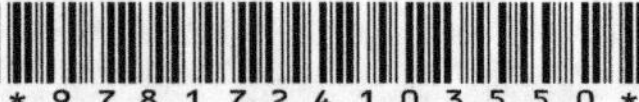